PRAISE FROM RESUME PLACE CLIE
(INCLUDING GOVERNMENT LAWY

"You created a resume for me in May 2014 (I got the job, thanks!). Is your company offering ALJ application assistance again this year? As I'm sure you've heard, OPM will be reopening testing within the next few months."

****

"The Resume Place was invaluable in my preparations for becoming an ALJ. They made the process simple and helped me understand exactly what OPM is looking for. Resume writing and assistance with the essays was invaluable. But the coaching was probably the most beneficial, as it prepared me for every stage in the ALJ application process. Thank you, Nicole!"

****

"The *ALJ Writing Guide* simplified the process for me. As a lawyer, there are so many things that you can write about yourself. But the *ALJ Writing Guide* walks you through each step, breaking down examples of what OPM is looking for in the ALJ application process. I could not have successfully completed the ALJ application process without this invaluable tool."

****

"Developing strong narratives to address the competencies and document your experience is not something we do every day. The narratives account for 50 points of your score and you need at least 40 to get on the register. You need around 60 points to be competitive. You are two-thirds of the way there if your narratives are good.

A competitive written application is the only part of the process under your exclusive control. Don't waste time – getting the help you need can be a deciding factor. The coaching will give you confidence as you go through the remaining process. Do yourself a favor. Do your loved ones a favor (you will torture them less if you get professional help). Retaining the coaching services of The Resume Place was the best money I spent on the process."

****

"I will recommend your services to EVERYONE. You have been great."

****

"I really appreciate your excellent advice and efficiency in helping me."

****

"I want to thank you for everything. If I get invited for an interview, it will only be because of your hard work and expertise! … I was blessed to get the best!"

ALJ Writing Guide 2nd Edition

The Resume Place, Inc.
1012 Edmondson Avenue, Catonsville, MD 21228
Phone: 888-480-8265
www.resume-place.com
Email: resume@resume-place.com

Printed in the United States of America

ALJ Writing Guide:
Application Writing and Test Preparation for Federal Administrative Law Judge Candidates
ISBN 13: 978-0-9846671-9-2
ISBN 10: 0-9846671-9-9

We have been careful to provide accurate federal job search information in this book, but it is possible that errors and omissions may have been introduced.

Sample Resumes: Sample resumes are real but fictionalized. All federal applicants have given permission for their resumes to be used as samples for this publication. Privacy policy is strictly enforced.

PUBLICATION TEAM:
Cover and Interior Page Design: Paulina Chen
Copyeditor: Pam Sikora

TABLE OF CONTENTS

INTRODUCTION

Thought to possess one of the best jobs in government, Administrative Law Judges (ALJs) typically hear entitlement cases but can also hear cases that fall into other categories, such as enforcement actions, regulatory cases, and contract disputes. Although case quotas can be high, especially for ALJs who hear and decide Social Security claims,[1] ALJs have no direct supervisors or subordinates, and are not subject to typical performance appraisal activities.[2]

With basic pay from $107,000 to $160,300 per year,[3] and locality pay which adds up to 25 (e.g., Boston, Chicago, Detroit) or even 35 percent (San Francisco), Administrative Law (AL) pay is commensurate with the Senior Executive Service (SES). ALJs are paid through a system separate from the General Schedule (GS) and SES. ALJs are neither subject to performance evaluations nor eligible for bonuses or other monetary awards.

For most Americans, an ALJ is the highest-ranking government official they will ever encounter. Although the public may not understand the difference between a judge in a Federal courthouse and the one who hears disability claims, legal

---

1 In Association of Administrative Law Judges, Judicial Council No. 1, IFPTE, AFL-CIO & CLC, et al. v. Commissioner, No. 14-1953, January 23, 2015, the U.S. Court of Appeals for the Seventh Circuit affirmed a district court's order dismissing plaintiffs' complaint alleging interference with decisional independence. The Seventh Circuit agreed that the Civil Service Reform Act precluded the ALJ union's claim that caseload goals imposed by the SSA chief ALJ violated the Administrative Procedure Act. Nor did the CSRA prohibit bona fide production increases, or incidental changes in working conditions occasioned by the new caseload goal. The new scheduled hearings benchmark for SSA was officially implemented on October 1, 2015. For more information about ALJ workloads at SSA, see the Administrative Law Judge Work Analysis Study, dated November 12, 2015, at https://drive.google.com/file/d/0B2kAAfgH45ClZjRGejdwSkwyNXc/view?pli=1.

2 See generally, http://ssaconnect.com/tfiles/ALJ-Overview.pdf.

3 https://www.opm.gov/policy-data-oversight/pay-leave/salaries-wages/pay-executive-order-2016-adjustments-of-certain-rates-of-pay.pdf.

professionals are of course aware that ALJs are different. What applicants may not fully appreciate is that ALJ applications are treated differently from other adjudicatory positions. While there are also Claims Examiners, Hearing Officers, Immigration Judges, Administrative Patent Judges and Boards of Contract Appeals Judges, ALJs are assigned their own, special job series. Series 0935 ALJs are not selected in the same manner as Attorney-Advisors (0905 series, Excepted Service positions), nor are they equivalent to other agency adjudicatory roles.

Federal ALJs are appointed to a register by Office of Personnel Management (OPM). Their selection for this roster is achieved through a rigorous, competitive examination process. ALJs are ultimately hired by an agency through a statutorily mandated, merit-based process. Subsequent service to this agency is subject to rules that preserve the ALJ's integrity, independence, and insulation from agency influence. They derive their power and judicial independence from the Administrative Procedure Act. They are like Federal trial judges in terms of tenure and compensation,[4] and otherwise serve as the functional equivalent of Federal trial judges.[5]

ALJs are assigned to more than 30 different agencies. The Social Security Administration (SSA) is by far the largest employer of ALJs, with more than 1,500 ALJs who adjudicate over 700,000 cases each year. Two other agencies with large numbers of Administrative Law Judges are the U.S. Department of Labor and the National Labor Relations Board, with about 60 each. The remaining ALJs work for agencies with as few as one or only a handful of judges.

Although all Administrative Law Judges are assigned to specific agencies, under an OPM program, ALJs from one agency can be assigned to hear cases for another agency when caseloads warrant.

Broadly, there are three categories of matters heard by ALJs: regulatory cases (economic regulation of rates and services); entitlement cases (determining claims based upon disability or death); and enforcement cases (under statutes and regulations relating to health, safety or other significant regulatory concerns). Regulatory cases include, for example, rate cases as directed by the Federal Energy Regulatory Commission. Entitlement cases include disability benefits claims under the Social Security Act, as well as workers compensation benefits cases under the Longshoremen and Harbor Workers Compensation Act. Enforcement cases may include, for example, mine safety cases heard by judges of the Mine Safety and Health Review Commission, workplace safety cases heard by judges of the Occupational Safety and Health Review Commission, and aviation safety cases heard by judges of the National Transportation Safety Board.

> ALJs are assigned to more than 30 different agencies. The Social Security Administration (SSA) is by far the largest employer of ALJs, with more than 1,500 ALJs.

4 Butz v. Economou, 438 U.S. 478 (1978).

5 Federal Maritime Com'n v. South Carolina State Ports Authority, 535 U.S. 743 (2002); see also, Rhode Island Dept. of Environmental Management v. United States, 304 F.3d 31(1st Cir. 2002) (Department of Labor ALJs are functionally equivalent to Federal District Judges).

The cases an ALJ hears depend on the employing agency. U.S. Department of Labor ALJs hear cases that range from whistleblower fraud to compensation claims brought by government contractors injured abroad. Federal Energy Regulatory Commission ALJs conduct hearings to ascertain the justness and reasonableness of utility rates and practices. Department of Agriculture ALJs conduct, among other things, enforcement proceedings relating to animal welfare.

Many active Administrative Law Judges will soon reach retirement age. Over the next 10 years, hundreds of ALJ positions will become available. SSA in particular, is in dire need of additional ALJs. Presently, over 90 percent of all ALJs hear only disability cases.

Soon, the Federal Administrative Law Judge announcement will reopen for all U.S. citizens, as it has done in 2009 and 2013. Although one more group of selectees is still being brought aboard from the 2013 examination process, this is the final group, and a new announcement will be posted soon. Once the new examination has been administered, those on the old register will need to reapply to the new announcement, and to begin preparing or updating their application materials now.

For ready access to ALJ postings, use the Advanced Search feature on USAJOBS.gov, and enter "0935" in the series number search field. It is also helpful to set up or update your USAJOBS.gov account now, and include a saved daily search for series 0935 positions. Also watch OPM's website, at https://www.opm.gov/news, for news releases related to the upcoming ALJ exam. In 2013, OPM released news of the upcoming announcement approximately one month ahead of time. In 2009, only two weeks' notice was provided.

Finally, put yourself in the correct frame of mind before you begin to prepare your application materials. Take a look at Professor Morell E. Mullins' *Manual for Administrative Law Judges*, at http://digitalcommons.pepperdine.edu/naalj/vol23/iss3/1, published by the National Association of Administrative Law Judiciary in collaboration with Pepperdine University. The ALJ Manual is one of its most popular papers. Other ALJ Manuals are available online or can be found by searching Google Books. The Administrative Law and Regulatory Practice Section of the ABA is also helpful. Its *Guide to Federal Agency Adjudication*, now in its second edition, by Jeffrey B. Litwak, is available for sale on the ABA's website (http://shop.americanbar.org/eBus/Store/ProductDetails.aspx?productId=213714) as well as through Amazon.com.

HISTORY OF THE ALJ APPLICATION

As of this writing, it is not possible to predict what process the 2016 ALJ announcement will impose, but having undergone a major overhaul in 2013, and in the absence of any indication that the 2013 process may be abandoned, the examination one sees in 2016 could resemble its predecessor. Though no one is allowed priority access to the application's requirements, testing processes or questions, the minimum requirements for service as a Federal ALJ are known—they remain the same. Candidates need to submit a resume and also demonstrate that they meet the position's minimum experience requirements—a full seven (7) years of qualifying litigation and/or administrative law experience as a licensed attorney.

The 2009 ALJ Selection Process

In 2009, applicants were required to submit a resume plus eight (8) narratives, two (2) setting forth their qualifying litigation and/or administrative law experience, and six (6) more, providing examples of accomplishments responsive to six (6) defined judicial competencies. Successful applicants were then invited to attend an in-person testing process and interview. Following this, applicants who attained a certain minimum score were invited to join the ALJ Register. Thereafter, agency hires were drawn from the highest scoring candidates on the register who had previously indicated a willingness to serve in the designated geographic location. Applicants who were overly selective in their choice of locales found job offers few and far between. Meanwhile, those who had indicated in their original ALJ application a willingness to serve anywhere were more likely to be hired from the register. After hire, and service in a less than convenient location, ALJs could seek transfer closer to home.

The 2013 ALJ Selection Process

The year 2013 brought big changes to the ALJ application and testing process:

- ✦ The number of judicial competencies swelled from six (6) to thirteen (13), none of which were defined in the announcement, though the initial set had been defined in 2009.

✦ The application required a resume, two (2) qualifications narratives documenting the applicant's litigation and/or administrative law experience, and an optional case listing of up to six (6) cases. Competency narratives were no longer a part of the application itself.

✦ Qualified applicants were invited to participate in online testing. This consisted of (a) participating in an avatar-driven situational judgment test; (b) preparing a writing sample in response to an online question; and (c) completing an experience assessment (questionnaire). Some narrative writing was required, but it was less onerous than in 2009.[1]

✦ Those who scored highly enough on the online component were invited to attend a proctored written demonstration (sample decision writing) and complete a logic-based measurement test. The logic test, reportedly, contained questions similar to those administered by other Federal hiring authorities in law enforcement or investigative positions, or even the multi-state portion of the bar exam.

✦ Finally, candidates participated in an hour-long, in-person, structured interview, conducted by three sitting or retired ALJs.

Challenges to be Addressed in 2016 and Beyond

A valuable overview of the challenges facing SSA and its efforts to attract and retain sufficient numbers of qualified ALJs is contained in the September 2015 SSA Office of the Inspector General (OIG) Audit Report, *The Social Security Administration's Efforts to Eliminate the Hearings Backlog*.[2] During the investigation, SSA's Office of Disability Adjudication and Review (ODAR) managers told OIG investigators that their most important initiative was hiring additional ALJs. SSA's hearing backlog includes more than one million claims, and is not likely to improve until at least fiscal year (FY) 2017.

According to the Audit Report, in FYs 2007 through 2013, ODAR increased the number of available ALJs from about 1,000 to 1,350. But by March 2015, its numbers dropped below 1,250. Although ODAR planned to hire 400 new ALJs in FYs 2013 and 2014, it added only 100. In FY 2015, it hoped to hire 250 new ALJs, but lowered that projection to 200, as of August 2015.[3] Meanwhile, ODAR was expecting to lose about 100 ALJs during this same period.

Based on its backlogs and case filings, ODAR executives told the SSA OIG that its ideal would be to have 1,800–1,900 ALJs by FY 2018. In early 2015, a workgroup drawn from SSA, OPM, the Office of Management and Budget, the Department of Justice, and the Administrative Conference of the United States convened to find ways to eliminate roadblocks in ALJ hiring.

---

1 Applicants were not permitted to share test questions and answers, but multiple candidates reported that the practice of crafting accomplishment narratives proved helpful to them during the online exam.

2 http://oig.ssa.gov/sites/default/files/audit/full/pdf/A-12-15-15005.pdf.

3 At publication, final numbers were not yet available.

Relief ultimately came in the form of the Bipartisan Budget Act of 2015, which passed on November 2, 2015:

```
SEC. 846. <<NOTE: 42 USC 904 note.>>   EXPEDITED EXAMINATION OF ADMINISTRATIVE
LAW JUDGES.

(a) In General.--Notwithstanding any other provision of law, the Office of
Personnel Management shall, upon request of the Commissioner of Social
Security, expeditiously administer a sufficient number of competitive
examinations, as determined by the Commissioner, for the purpose
of identifying an adequate number of candidates to be appointed as
Administrative Law Judges under section 3105 of title 5, United States Code.
<<NOTE: Deadlines.>> The first such examination shall take place not later
than April 1, 2016 and other examinations shall take place at such time or
times requested by the Commissioner, but not later than December 31, 2022.
Such examinations shall proceed even if one or more individuals who took a
prior examination have appealed an adverse determination and one or more of
such appeals have not concluded, provided that--

     (1) the Commissioner of Social Security has made a determination that
     delaying the examination poses a significant risk that an adequate number
     of Administrative Law Judges will not be available to meet the need of the
     Social Security Administration to reduce or prevent a backlog of cases
     awaiting a hearing;

     (2) an individual whose appeal is pending is provided an option to continue
     their appeal or elects to take the new examination, in which case the
     appeal is considered vacated; and

     (3) an individual who decides to continue his or her appeal and who
     ultimately prevails in the appeal shall receive expeditious consideration
     for hire by the Office Personnel Management and the Commissioner of Social
     Security.

(b) Payment of Costs.--Notwithstanding any other provision of law, the
Commissioner of Social Security shall pay the full cost associated with each
examination conducted pursuant to subsection (a).
```

[Emphasis added.]

Because SSA will now drive the process, ALJ announcements could become more frequent. Or, examinations could be conducted on a rolling basis, in more locations. Other changes are possible, but at this time, none have been announced.

Although no ALJ announcement has been posted, all those who wish to be considered for hire in 2016 and beyond should prepare or update their ALJ application materials by the April 1, 2016 deadline referred to in the Bipartisan Budget Act. This advice applies to all those who may yet have appeals pending relative to the disposition of their 2013 applications, as well as those who may have earned a slot on the current register but have not been offered a position in the latest round of hires.

ALJ Application and Test procedures

Part 1 - Qualifications and Application

A. Qualifications and Your Federal Resume

The ALJ qualification requirements include:

✦ A full seven (7) years of experience as a licensed attorney preparing for, participating in, and/or reviewing formal hearings or trials involving litigation and/or administrative law at the Federal, State or local level;

✦ A professional license and authorization to practice law under the laws of a State, the District of Columbia, the Commonwealth of Puerto Rico, or any territorial court established under the U.S. Constitution; and

✦ Passing OPM's competitive examination process, during which the competencies essential to performing the work of an ALJ are tested.

What serves as qualifying experience? Per OPM, the types of cases handled must have been conducted *on the record* under procedures at least as formal as those prescribed by the Administrative Procedure Act (APA), set forth in 5 U.S.C. §§ 553–559. This would include cases heard pursuant to the very similar Model State Administrative Procedure Act (Model State APA).

The requisite experience can be gained in handling cases in which a complaint is filed with a court, or a charging document (e.g., indictment or information) was issued by a court, a grand jury, or appropriate military authority, and includes:

✦ Participating in settlement or plea negotiations in advance of trial;
✦ Preparing for trial and/or participating in trial of cases;
✦ Preparing opinions;
✦ Hearing cases;
✦ Participating in or conducting arbitration, mediation, or other alternative dispute resolution process approved by the court; or
✦ Participating in appeals related to the types of cases above.

Qualifying administrative law experience can be gained handling cases with a formal procedure before a governmental administrative body. This includes:

+ Participating in settlement negotiations in advance of hearing cases;
+ Preparing for hearing and/or participating in trial of cases;
+ Preparing opinions;
+ Hearing cases;
+ Participating in or conducting arbitration, mediation, or other alternative dispute resolution process approved by the administrative body; or
+ Participating in appeals related to the types of cases above.

Thus, an Attorney-Advisor employed by at the SSA Office of Disability Adjudication and Review (ODAR) who, as a practicing attorney, has done nothing apart from preparing ALJ opinions for seven (7) years, can qualify. A former judicial clerk who spent time drafting opinions for a state or Federal judge could count such time as well. Note that this experience must be gained after admission to the bar. Judicial clerkship experience which takes place before admission to the bar cannot be credited.

Meanwhile, experience with cases having no formal hearing procedure and uncontested cases involving misdemeanors, probate, domestic relations, or tort matters is not qualifying. Teaching trial practice skills while practicing law part time for seven (7) years does not qualify. Applicants must be able to document that their qualifying litigation and administrative law experience adds up to seven (7) full years of practice. If one's law practice extends beyond trial work to transactional law, government contracting, etc., the qualifying part of that work may or may not add up to the minimum amount. It is up to the candidate to demonstrate, unequivocally, that he or she possesses this minimum experience.

Although no specific resume format or content was prescribed by the 2013 ALJ announcement, the applicant ought to make sure that the resume itself confirms both the nature and amount of experience being relied upon to support the application. One should do so in addition to submitting the detailed narratives described below.

In preparing the resume, the candidate should fully describe the nature of the skills applied, and provide examples of accomplishments that show how he or she has applied various ALJ competencies to advance client or case disposition goals. Though these competencies will be tested and measured during the ALJ examination process, the application requires submission of a USAJOBS resume.

Applicants who are unfamiliar with the Federal hiring process should study the typical components and structure of a Federal resume. Resumes can be submitted either by using the online builder or by uploading a Word or PDF version. Applicants are encouraged to study the information requested in the online builder, and mimic the format if preparing an uploaded version. Federal resumes are much longer and more detailed than private sector resumes. They spell out with specificity one's job duties and functions, as well as relevant accomplishments. In most cases, this means preparing summaries of one's most relevant accomplishments that reflect upon the competencies required for the position.

Although OPM does not specify what must be included in an ALJ candidate's resume, applicants are well-advised to develop and include content to support both the minimum qualifying experience and substantive competencies required of a successful ALJ. When the hiring agency is asked to consider candidates for hire, agency hiring officials will review the resume (and case listing) before making a decision. Thus, the resume has two separate audiences. One (OPM) views the resume at the time of application to join the ALJ register; the other (typically, SSA) views the resume when the certification list is forwarded.

It is important to keep both audiences in mind when preparing your resume and including, among other things, information probative of all of the knowledge, skills, and abilities an ALJ needs. It should describe, for example, the numbers and type(s) of cases handled, case management experience, and expertise with medical, psychological, or disability issues. The resume should include examples of accomplishments demonstrating how the candidate has advanced client or institutional goals through the application of the thirteen (13) competencies.

Most Federal resumes place relevant work experience in the front. Meanwhile, education, certifications and licenses go in the back. The resume must list inclusive months and years of employment for each relevant job, plus hours per week. Salary is usually listed, but is not always required. Federal employees should list their series and grade. The resume must have an organized summary of relevant duties and responsibilities, responsive to the job announcement's minimum qualifications and competencies, followed by the accomplishment summaries. Next, list education and licensing information, including date of admission to the bar and bar number. Pro bono activities, professional associations, and publications follow, along with any meaningful awards.

A Federal resume is typically three (3) to five (5) pages long. It devotes more space to more recent jobs, less to older jobs, especially if the jobs are similar. There is no requirement to list every job you have held—but do list those that reflect relevant experience in fields relevant to the agency likely to hire you. Do include internships, clerkships, and fellowships. Specific tips for ALJ candidates (and legal candidates generally):

- ✦ Attorneys who have spent extended periods on their own, handling contract assignments for multiple law firms or contracting agencies, along with the occasional direct representation of a client, should think of themselves as solo practitioners, and organize these experiences as accomplishment summaries. The contracting agency can be reflected parenthetically at the end of an accomplishment paragraph.

- ✦ Unless military history involves the exercise of legal skills that reflect well on the ALJ competencies, candidates should not devote much space to this work experience. The history is informative, but much less important than the qualifying legal experience.

- ✦ The same goes for pre-legal experience. If it is completely unrelated, leave it out. Some candidates may have attended law school or joined the bar after working as a social worker, nurse, or paralegal. These jobs reflect relevant skills, but extensive detail is not required.

Sample "Before" and "After" resumes are reproduced on the following pages.

Magistrate James Charlemagne
403 Hogsmart Road ▪ Miles, Iowa 12345
(555) 555-1212 ▪ james@email.com

Objective

Seeking meaningful, challenging, and rewarding employment in the Federal Government where my over ten years of combined experience as an Assistant Prosecutor, Mediator, and Magistrate will be utilized in an environment where there is an opportunity for personal and professional growth.

Employment History

Magistrate, Trumpet County Common Pleas Court, General Division   **2007-present**

-Providing Administrative and Legal Support to the Judges of the Court of Common Pleas of Trumpet County, Iowa, in Criminal and Civil Matters, including Jury Instructions, Review and Recommendations on Pending Motions, Decision Making and Preparation of Judicial Opinions for the Judges.

-Presiding over Trials both to the Bench and to the Jury on Orders of Reference under Iowa Civil Rule 53 in all areas of Civil Law, including but not limited to: Personal Injury, Real Estate and Real Estate Foreclosure, Zoning and Planning, Labor Disputes, Breach of Contract, Mandamus, School Law, Employment Law, and Tax Collection.

-Conducting Hundreds of Pre-Trials both on Referred Cases and on behalf of the Trial Judges of the Trumpet County Common Pleas Court.

-Successfully Mediating Hundreds of Cases in the Court of Common Pleas in Dispute Areas including but not limited to: Personal Injury, Real Estate, Zoning and Planning, Foreclosure, Labor Disputes, Breach of Contract, and Worker's Compensation.

Assistant Prosecuting Attorney, Trumpet County Prosecutor's Office   **2000-2006**

-Counseled and Represented County Commissioners, Auditor, Board of Revision, Treasurer, Recorder, Clerk of Courts, Board of Health, Townships, and the Common Pleas Court in Trumpet County.

-Prosecuted Over One Thousand Delinquent Tax Foreclosures and Collections Cases and Represented Trumpet County in All Land Valuation Proceedings before the Iowa Board of Tax Appeals and the Trumpet County Court of Common Pleas.

-Co-Authored Trumpet County Regulations, Common Pleas Court Foreclosure Rules, Trumpet County Tourism Board by-laws, Bid Specifications for Public Projects, and Hundreds of Resolutions of the Trumpet County Board of Commissioners.

-Created Dispute Resolution and Administrative Hearing Procedure for County Board of Health and Handled Hundreds of Administrative Hearings.

-Actively Participated in Labor Negotiations on Behalf of Trumpet County.

-Litigated Many Cases involving Public Law on behalf of Trumpet County, including Land Use and Zoning, Tax, Land Valuations, Bankruptcy, Contract, Administrative Appeals, Public Nuisance, Prisoner Appeals, Personal Injury and Negligence.

-Practice Experience in District Court of Appeals, United States District Court of Iowa, Bankruptcy Court, Trumpet County Court of Common Pleas, Iowa State Personnel Board of Review, Iowa Board of Tax Appeals, and Municipal and County Courts.

-Authored Advisory Opinions to Local Public Officials, Subdivisions, and Agencies on Issues of Law and Fact and Provided Effective and Efficient General Counsel.

Solo Practicing Attorney, James Charlemagne, Attorney at Law   **1999-2006**

-Solo Practice with Experience in General Civil Practice, Bankruptcy, Collection, Criminal (through 2000), Domestic, Forcible Entry and Detainer, and Probate Matters.

Education

Admitted to the Iowa Bar, November 1999
Juris Doctor, Iowa University School of Law, May 1999
B.A., University of Iowa (English) May 1996

Social Activities

Vice President/ President-Elect, Trumpet County Bar Association.
Trumpet County Bar Association Executive Committee, 2007-2009.
Trumpet County Bar Association, 1999-present.
Recognized as a Mahoghany Valley MVP "40 Under 40" Award Recipient, 2007.
Iowa State Bar Association, 1999-present.
Iowa Association of Magistrates, 2007-present.
Treasurer, Trumpet County Young Democrats, 2004-2006.
Order of AHEPA, 2005-present.
Trumpet County Farm Bureau, 2007-present.
Associate Member, Trumpet County Township Association, 2005-present.
Volunteer, River Little League, Manager, Pro Bono Legal Counsel, 2002-2005.
Married since 2003 to Marjorie (Dunham) Charlemagne, no children.

RESUME SAMPLE 1: AFTER RESUME

JAMES CHARLEMAGNE
403 Hogsmart Road • Miles, Iowa 12345
515.555.1212 (m) • james@email.com
U.S. Citizen • Selective Service Registered

PROFESSIONAL EXPERIENCE

MAGISTRATE	01/2007–Present
County Common Pleas Court, Miles, Iowa 12345	$75,000/yr
Contact Supervisor: Yes, Hon. W. Wyatt Earp, 515.123.4567	40+ hrs/wk

PRESIDE OVER 60+ HEARINGS AND TRIALS ON THE RECORD and MANAGE A DOCKET of 600+ CASES PER YEAR as a trial court magistrate in a court with general jurisdiction. Also, hear and decide preliminary motions, discovery motions, motions to exclude, summary judgment motions, motions concerning the admission of expert testimony, dispositive motions, motions concerning the jury, and post trial motions.

RESEARCH/ANALYZE ISSUES OF LAW AND FACT; MAKE BINDING DECISIONS. Review briefs, research law, interpret and apply statutes, regulations and codes, decide cases, and enter 300+ judgments per year on disputed matters for the Court. Analyze and interpret complex matters in both civil and criminal cases. Render clear oral and written decisions in sometimes highly difficult and contentious disputes.

POSSESS A COMPOSED AND PROFESSIONAL JUDICIAL TEMPERAMENT. Preside over difficult cases while maintaining a professional demeanor; at all times preserve the decorum of the courtroom, free of personal and societal prejudices and consistent with my judicial authority. Handle rancorous or emotionally difficult issues with calmness and compassion for the lives and interests at stake. Through effective dispute resolution techniques, I mediate and settle 300+ cases per year.

JUDICIAL MANAGEMENT includes personal injury, worker's compensation, real estate foreclosures, collections, breaches of contracts, judgment enforcement, zoning, and election disputes. Manage my own docket of general civil cases referred under Iowa Civil Rule 53 for disposition by trial.

Representative Accomplishments:

• RESOLVED LARGE COMMERCIAL LEASE DISPUTE between 2 nationwide corporations; 1,000 jobs were at stake. Sub-lessee of former retail property earned profits not properly accounted for in rent when payments were made. Following major ruling for landlord, presided over settlement talks leading to sale of property to tenant and preservation of 1,000 jobs in region with depressed local economy.

• PRESIDED OVER 1,000+ HOME FORECLOSURES in County Common Pleas Court. Successfully mediated 100s of cases involving homeowners unable to pay mortgages. Mediations have provided diverse, distressed community members a second chance at home ownership.

• RENDERED WELL-ANALYZED TRIAL COURT OPINION IN COMPLEX CASE. Held that new collateral source abrogation statute did not overrule prior cases limiting medical expenses to amounts actually accepted in full payment for medical services because the statute did not address evidence of write-offs by providers. My approach was subsequently adopted by Iowa's Supreme Court.

• REWROTE RULES OF COURT for County Common Pleas Court governing the procedures applicable to the 1,500 real estate foreclosures filed each year, following adoption of new Iowa state law.

ASSISTANT PROSECUTING ATTORNEY   08/2000–12/2006
Trumpet County, Mars, Iowa 00000 $58,000/yr
Contact Supervisor: Yes, Hon. Dennis Mennis, 515.098.7654   40+ hrs/wk

ASSISTANT PROSECUTOR, Civil Division of the Trumpet County Prosecutor's Office. Worked independently but as part of a team that worked together to provide high quality in-house and courtroom legal representation to elected officials and agencies. Work was 50% litigation related.

TRIED NUMEROUS CASES ON THE RECORD in court and before Administrative Law Judges. Prosecuted 1,000+ tax foreclosure cases, handled 200+ tax assessment hearings, and prosecuted nuisance abatement cases. Represented County Board of Health in all of its administrative and litigation related enforcement actions, many of which involved negotiation and cooperation with Iowa EPA and U.S. EPA.

REPRESENTED COUNTY COMMISSIONERS. Handled daily duties as legal counsel for County with 220,000+ residents. Addressed human resource and employment/unemployment matters, collective bargaining issues, public record requests, open meeting compliance, and administrative and authoritative functions of County.

Representative Accomplishments:

• OVERSAW IMPLEMENTATION OF ADMINISTRATIVE HEARING PROCEDURE in Health District to enforce new regulations without compromising citizens' rights to due process. Navigated Board of Health through challenging septic tank crisis in which Iowa EPA mandated that County adopt new home sewage treatment system (HSTS) regulations, forcing thousands of homeowners to update existing septic systems, costing each of them thousands of dollars and causing great anger and emotional distress in the community. New local procedure calmed nerves and satisfied EPA.

• WON APPEAL AGAINST DEATH ROW INMATE involving his untimely challenge of a 10-year-old court costs judgment. Convicted murderer pled indigence to avoid garnishment of commissary account of over $5,000. Afterwards I facilitated adoption of new procedures whereby the Clerk garnishes the accounts of all incarcerated felons. The procedure returns thousands of dollars per year to law enforcement.

• SUCCESSFULLY DEFENDED COMMISSIONERS IN CONTENTIOUS SUIT BY VISITORS BUREAU. In highly sensitive, public, and complex lawsuit Trumpet County Convention and Visitors Bureau sued the Board of County Commissioners for substantial tax monies it claimed it was owed. Following a favorable settlement for a tiny fraction of this amount, the insolvent Bureau disbanded and I successfully organized, with the cooperation of local businesses, the charter of a new and successful private corporation to handle the County's tourism affairs.

ATTORNEY   11/1999–12/2006
Law Offices of James Charlemagne, Miles, Iowa 12345   10 hrs/wk

MAINTAINED SOLO LITIGATION PRACTICE while also maintaining full time employment in government. Handled general civil litigation, contested probate matters, bankruptcy cases, collections, and evictions. Represented individual and corporate clients and provided competent and cost efficient representation in matters of both simple and complex litigation. Consistent with legal requirements, ceased private practice of law upon accepting appointment as full time Magistrate in the Court of Common Pleas.

EDUCATION

J.D. June 1999, Iowa University School of Law (90 Semester Hours; GPA: 3.6/4.0)
B.A. June 1996, University of Iowa (English; GPA: 3.5/4.0)

LICENSE

Iowa Bar, Member No. 123456 (November 1999–present)

AFFILIATIONS/AWARDS

Member, Iowa State Bar Association
Vice President and President Elect, Trumpet County Bar Association
Member, Iowa Association of Magistrates
Member, Order of AHEPA (American Hellenic Educational Progressive Association)
Member, Trumpet County Farm Bureau
Member and Past Honoree, MVP 20/30 Club
Associate Member, Trumpet County Township Association
Member, Trumpet County Soil and Water Conservation District

Included among those awarded 2007 "Mahogany Valley 40 Under 40," honoring outstanding professionals who have contributed positively to the community. Successfully sponsored five additional young professionals for the award, 2008–2010.

PROFESSIONAL REFERENCES

Hon. W. Wyatt Earp
Trumpet County Common Pleas, Presiding Judge
Phone Number: 515.123.4567

Hon. Peter J. Principle
Trumpet County Common Pleas, Court Judge
Phone Number: 515.345.6789

Selim Suleiman
District Board of Elections and Ethics, Executive Director
Phone Number: 515.456.7890

Paul Hertz
Trumpet County Commissioner
Phone Number: 515.567.8901

MICHAEL FOUCAULT
ATTORNEY AT LAW

WORK EXPERIENCE

FOUCAULT LAW OFFICES, LLC   2008 - PRESENT
Managing Member
Foucault Law Offices, LLC is a Cincinnati-based law firm focused on providing superior client service and sound legal advice to help our clients overcome challenges and realize opportunities.

CORPS EXPERTS, LLC   2010 - PRESENT
Principal
Core Experts, LLC is a consulting firm that combines military and legal expertise to advise business owners and attorneys nationwide on military personnel issues.

OFFICE OF CONGRESSMAN DANIEL DEFERT   2006 - 2008
Counsel / Military Fellow
Served as an advisor to Chairman Defert on National Security issues. My advisory portfolio included defense, intelligence, border security, and veterans' affairs. I had daily interaction with Members of Congress, Professional Staff Members, constituents, industry representatives and policy organizations. Also responsible for drafting legislation, preparing memoranda for committee hearings, and writing talking points for the Congressman.

UNITED STATES MARINE CORPS   1997 - PRESENT
Lieutenant Colonel, United States Marine Corps Reserve
Eighteen years of active and reserve military experience serving in the United States and abroad with military and high level civilian staffs in time-critical, high-stress environments. Significant experience serving in both command and staff roles.

EDUCATION

GEORGETOWN UNIVERSITY SCHOOL OF LAW   2007
Juris Doctor, Concentrations Awarded in Criminal Law and Litigation with Honors

UNIVERSITY OF DAYTON   1998
Bachelor of Arts, History

BAR ADMISSIONS

OHIO   2008

DISTRICT OF COLUMBIA   2010

NEW YORK STATE   2013

Awards and Honors

Major General Harold W. Chase Prize Essay "Boldness and Daring Award"
Awarded second place in an annual writing contest in a professional journal. Article published in the *Marine Corps Gazette* in August, 2006.

Presidential Management Fellowship Finalist (Class of 2006)
Selected from over 3,200 applicants nationwide for a two-year executive branch post-graduate school fellowship. I ultimately declined appointment as a Presidential Management Fellow to accept a Congressional Fellowship.

Dean's List, Georgetown University School of Law
Spring Semester 2006, Fall Semester 2006, Spring Semester 2007.

Community Service

Board of Trustees, "The Northeastern Semper Fidelis Foundation"   2004 - 2007
Founded a federally recognized 501(c)(3) charity to help meet the needs of local Marines returning from combat. Current assets in excess of $350,000 being used to provide short and long term care to local veterans in need.

Cincinnati Bar Association, "The Three R's Program"   2005 - 2006
Volunteered teaching Constitutional Law to high school juniors at an inner-city public school as part of a Bar Association outreach program.

Additional Information

Active Top Secret/SCI Security Clearance (re-adjudicated in 2014)
Member: Ohio State Bar Association, Cincinnati Bar Association

Resume Sample 2: After Resume

MICHAEL FOUCAULT

111 Clermont Road, Cincinnati, OH 45201
123-456-9876 | Foucault@lawmail.com
Veteran's Preference: 5 Point | Top Secret/SCI Security Clearance

---

PROFESSIONAL EXPERIENCE

MANAGING PARTNER • TRIAL ATTORNEY
01/2008–Present*

Foucault Law Offices, LLC • Cincinnati, OH
55 Hours/Week

Supervisor: Self-Employed
$125,000/Year

ENGAGE IN LITIGATION, FULL-TIME: Prepare and manage complex personal injury cases for trial from start to finish, including pre-trial, trial (jury and non-jury), post-trial motions and appeals. Represent injured plaintiffs before Ohio trial and appellate courts, U.S. District Courts (N.D. and S.D. Ohio), U.S. Court of Appeals (6th Cir.). Handle personal injury cases, including motor torts, premises liability, medical negligence, Federal Tort Claims Act cases and claims; and claims/cases against disability insurers. Assess evidence to develop litigation options and strategies. Manage discovery. Manage all aspects of cases and claims, from case evaluation and intake to resolution, via negotiated settlement or other alternative dispute resolution process. Enforce settlements and judgments, as necessary.

REPRESENT CLIENTS WITH COMPLEX MEDICAL ISSUES: Develop issues ranging from repetitive strain (carpal tunnel) to traumatic injuries (including brain injuries), autoimmune diseases, surgical injuries, cancer, and others. Develop psychiatric and psychological injury claims, including Post Traumatic Stress Disorder. Assemble complete client histories and records; liaise effectively with medical, psychiatric, psychological and rehabilitation and/or physical therapy experts; and support the preparation of expert reports and testimony establishing causation and disability claims and associated economic damages. Assist clients in confirming complex personal, medical and employment histories, overcome challenges to cases, and realize opportunities for improved case outcomes. Build and maintain strong client relationships throughout the full process of claims resolution, from advising and negotiating settlements to preparing them for deposition and trial, and advocating on their behalf throughout.

RESEARCH & ANALYZE COMPLEX LITIGATION ISSUES: Develop and apply expert knowledge of a number of areas of substantive and procedural law, including state and federal rules of evidence, discovery, privilege, immunities, tort law (common law and statutory), and relevant aspects of employment and insurance law. For claims that must first be presented before administrative law judges, apply knowledge of agency hearing processes and decision-making. Conduct legal research and brief issues as required.

PREPARE LITIGATION DOCUMENTS: Prepare detailed legal analyses, memoranda, and court filings. Draft complex documents (e.g., complaints, pre- and post-trial briefs, discovery requests, practice motions, legal memoranda, correspondence, affidavits, exhibits) to support legal arguments. As may be required, prepare proposed findings of fact and rulings of law.

MANAGE LAW PRACTICE: Supervise two attorneys. Lead and manage practice, firm operations, and business management activities. Ensure compliance with all professional responsibilities, including conflicts, privacy, confidentiality, records retention, continuing education, reporting, and communications. Maintain case management tools and technology to ensure deadlines are met and cases effectively managed and prioritized.

Selected Accomplishments:

—Have personally litigated on behalf of hundreds of tort plaintiffs and claimants. Have tried multiple $1M+ claims for catastrophic injury and loss related to medical malpractice, products liability and premises liability (food poisoning; dog bite; deck collapse).

—Briefed and argued significant state court appeal related to the use of expert medical testimony to support use of "recovered memory" evidence of childhood sexual abuse.

—Sought after speaker on trial practice skills. Regularly conduct continuing education classes and serve on panels on behalf of Cleveland Bar Association and Ohio State Bar.

—Contributed chapter on medical evidence to leading Ohio trial practice book (in publication).

INCLUDES QUALIFYING TIME OFF AS ACTIVE DUTY MILITARY, DEPLOYED 08/2010–03/2012.

DOD CONGRESSIONAL FELLOW (EQ. TO GS-13)   08/2006–01/2008
Office of Representative Daniel Defert   50 Hours/Week
U.S. House of Representatives, Washington, DC
Supervisor: Raymond Roussel (202-111-1111)

Nominated and Board-selected as a DOD Congressional Fellow by the United States Marine Corps. Further selected from 2006 Fellows Class to serve in the Office of the then-Chair of the House Permanent Select Committee on Intelligence and senior member of the House Armed Services Committee.

MILITARY FELLOW, COUNSEL, & LEGISLATIVE ASSISTANT: Advised the Congressman on defense and national security issues. Portfolio included civil-military interaction, intelligence, border security, and veterans' affairs. Regularly briefed the Congressman, other Members of Congress and Congressional Committees, professional staff, constituents, industry representatives and policy organizations.

RESEARCH AND ANALYSIS: Effectively managed a constant flow of information and provided outstanding real-time research and analysis of issues relevant to the Office's legislative agenda, including the legislative and budget processes and oversight duties. Assessed the consequences of legislative and procedural options.

TEAMWORK & COMMUNICATION: Worked effectively with top government decision makers, including senior members of the DOD, on policy and acquisition issues. Built long-term relationships and sought out appropriate contacts.

LEGAL WRITING: Drafted legislation, prepared memoranda for hearings, and wrote talking points for the Congressman. Collaborated with other staff to ensure an integrative approach.

WORKLOAD MANAGEMENT: Utilized excellent time-management and organization skills to ensure that urgent issues were handled in a timely manner and balanced with other Office needs.

Selected Accomplishments:

—Advised the Congressman on a wide range of substantive issues, most notably the National Defense Authorization Act.

—Performance review cited my work as "among the best this year on Capitol Hill," and acknowledged my "unmatched ability to convey strategic communication message to Members of Congress and professional staff."

MILITARY EXPERIENCE

UNITED STATES MARINE CORPS

Executive Officer (Lt. Col.)   12/2014–Present
4th Light Armored Reconnaissance Battalion, U.S. Marine Corps Reserves   5 Hours/Week

CHIEF OF STAFF & SECOND IN COMMAND of a 1,500-Marine battalion with companies in six states. Lead and manage 30 field and company grade officers and senior enlisted Marines.

Operations Officer (Major)   03/2012–12/2014
2d Air Naval Gunfire Liaison Company, U.S. Marine Corps Reserves   5 Hours/Week

MANAGED DAY-TO-DAY OPERATIONS and training of unit. Supervised 10 staff; planned for training, exercises, and operational employment. Assessed/addressed training readiness.

Future Operations Officer (Major)   08/2010–03/2012
22d Marine Expeditionary Unit, U.S. Marine Corps   70 Hours/Week

DEPLOYED ACTIVE-DUTY OFFICER supporting Libya and Middle East operations. Planned theater security cooperation events; coordinated contingency operations with U.S. Navy Fleet and Combatant Command staffs. Briefed general/flag officer commanders and SES members.

Officer in Charge (Captain)   01/2003–01/2008
Forward Operating Command Post   70 Hours/Week
Combined Joint Task Force – Consequence Management, U.S. Marine Corps

DEPLOYED OVERSEAS. Led multinational staff during initial phase of the war in Iraq, coordinating unit response to ballistic missile alerts to monitor impact and intercept sites for evidence of enemy use of Weapons of Mass Destruction (WMDs).

EDUCATION

JURIS DOCTORATE (J.D.), 05/2007
Georgetown University Law Center • Washington, DC
—Concentration Areas: Criminal Law and Litigation, with Honors.
—Honors: Dean's List (2006-2008); CALI Excellence Award for the Future (2008)

BACHELOR OF ARTS (B.A.), 08/1998
University of Dayton • Dayton, Ohio
—Major: History

BAR ADMISSIONS

Ohio, Admitted October 15, 2008 • Bar #1234567
District of Columbia, Admitted June 25, 2010 • Bar #2345678
New York State, Admitted June 26, 2013 • Bar #345678

Admitted to practice before the United States District Court, Northern and Southern Districts of Ohio; and United States Court of Appeals for the Sixth Circuit

---

AWARDS & HONORS

Major General Harold W. Chase Prize Essay "Boldness and Daring Award." Awarded second place in an annual writing contest in a professional journal. Article published in the *Marine Corps Gazette* (08/2006).

Presidential Management Fellowship Finalist (Class of 2006). Selected from over 3,200 applicants nationwide for a two-year executive branch post-graduate school fellowship. Accepted DOD Congressional Fellowship instead.

Navy and Marine Corps Commendation Medals (2001, 2004, 2012, 2014) • Navy and Marine Corps Achievement Medal (2006) • Joint Meritorious Unit Award (2005) • Meritorious Unit Citations (2002, 2005, 2014) • Selected Marine Corps Reserve Medals (2007, 2010, 2013) • National Defense Service Medal (2001) • Global War on Terrorism Expeditionary Medal (2003) • Global War on Terrorism Service Medal (2005) • Sea Service Deployment Ribbons (2001, 2003, 2012) • Armed Forces Reserve Medals (2005, 2012) • NATO Medal (2013)

COMMUNITY SERVICE & MEMBERSHIPS

Board of Trustees • The Northeastern Semper Fidelis Foundation • 2004–2007
Instructor, "The Three R's Program" • Cleveland Bar Association • 2005–2006
Volunteer • Habitat for Humanity • 2009–2012
Member • American Bar Association, Litigation Section
Member • Ohio Bar Association
Member • Cleveland Bar Association

B. Litigation and Administrative Narratives

Applicants must demonstrate that they meet the position's minimum experience requirements—a full seven (7) years of qualifying litigation and/or administrative law experience as a licensed attorney, preparing for, participating in, and/or reviewing formal hearings or trials involving litigation and/or administrative law at the Federal, State or local level. Applicants must also read the online instructions carefully. An otherwise polished qualifications narrative may be deemed insufficient if the required specificity of timeframe and percentages of time spent carrying out qualifying activities are not provided. The 2013 questionnaire expressly warned applicants:

> When you are describing your experience, it is extremely important that you provide sufficient detail to show that you have completed, in the aggregate, a full seven years of qualifying experience. Therefore, you must quantify the time associated with any claimed experience in terms of the specific dates it was acquired, including the month and year for the start and end dates, such as May 2006-December 2006. Also, if you provide an example of qualifying experience that overlaps with other non-qualifying experience, you must provide the percentage of time spent on each type of work.

Accordingly, a successful candidate might state:

Litigation Experience

I began working for Smith & Jones, a civil litigation firm with about 75 attorneys in Washington, D.C. in November 2002. My first five years were spent as an associate attorney researching complex legal questions and preparing litigation memos, pleadings, briefs and discovery requests and responses as a member of the firm's construction litigation team. This team pursued and directed the pursuit of litigation nationwide, in both state and Federal courts, and in the D.C. courts. We litigated cases involving crane collapses and building structural failures.

I was involved in almost every aspect of the firm's cases, from case review and theory development, to jury selection and case strategy development, as well as pretrial setup consult with the judge, clerk, and bailiff, to ensure the presentation of evidence progressed smoothly throughout the trial. Most of my work revolved around preparing for and attending depositions, engaging in document discovery, reviewing discovery documents, and liaising with teams of document reviewers who assisted us with our cases.

After the first five years, I progressed in my fulltime pursuit of Federal and state court litigation, participating more fully as a member of the firm's complex torts trial team. I conducted investigations to obtain facts about cases, studied legal precedents and participated in trial preparations. I drafted memoranda of law, pleadings, responsive pleadings, witness affidavits, jury charges, advisory memoranda for other attorneys, and appellate briefs. I was part of the litigation team trying personal injury cases, product liability cases, fraud cases, mass tort cases, environmental law cases, business law cases, as well as nursing home cases. I picked or helped pick juries, listened to and analyzed witness testimony, and gave advice about secondary questions. I examined witnesses. I served as second chair attorney most of the time, but did serve as first chair for two individual products liability claims. I also participated in appeals, working on about two appeals per month, including some that set precedent on various aspects of tort law and trial practice.

Beginning in August 2007 I also began to teach law, part time, at XYZ University, in their civil litigation clinical program. For the next 18 months, or until January 2009, I devoted approximately 25% of my time to teaching and the remaining 75% of my time to actively litigating cases at my firm.

I left the firm in January 2009, shortly before joining the Social Security Administration's Office of Disability Adjudication and Review (ODAR) as an Attorney-Advisor.

Administrative Law Experience

Since February 2009, I have engaged full time in the practice of administrative law as an Attorney-Advisor with the Social Security Administration's Office of Disability Adjudication and Review (ODAR) in San Francisco, California. I carry out a variety of activities relating to the hearings and appeals process in cases brought pursuant to Title II and Title XVI of the Social Security Act. I have prepared opinions, advised and assisted Administrative Law Judges in preparation of decisions, engaged in post-hearing development, and participated in other post-hearing actions. I have performed research; identified and briefed issues in cases; reviewed legal documents in preparation for writing decisions; interpreted statutes, regulations, and previous decisions; and reviewed past decisions by the Appeals Council in preparation for writing current decisions.

I have reviewed legal issues and analyzed Federal and state laws on matters relating to Social Security programs to make formal recommendations. I have also analyzed my caseload and set priorities among the assignments to ensure that my workload is managed appropriately and within Agency guidelines. Since joining ODAR, I have drafted decisions in approximately 1,100 cases. I have consistently, with very few exceptions, met my monthly benchmark for cases by 100% or greater.

Of my work as an attorney with ODAR, one of the ALJs wrote in January 2011, "You have written quite a number of affirmation decisions of mine, all of which have been very good, the latest of which was especially comprehensive and excellent. You obviously put a lot of effort into your work and it shows." On another occasion, a different ALJ wrote, "Each decision is well written with a detailed credibility analysis. Thank you—you are doing great work." At least two of my cases were affirmed on appeal and have been published.

Notice that the candidate includes both month and year and, when describing non-qualifying experience, clarifies the percentage of time devoted to that activity.

C. Listing of Significant Litigation and/or Administrative Law Cases (Optional)

The 2013 ALJ announcement specified the format to be used to cite and discuss up to six (6) of the most significant litigation and/or formal administrative law cases the applicant has prepared, participated in, and/or reviewed. The application required the case listing document to be uploaded as a separate document in the "Other" document category listed in the drop-down menu of Application Manager. Although these cases were not scored as part of the ALJ examination, they would be used later on in the selection process. The cases were provided to hiring agencies with the candidate's resume if his or her name appeared on the ALJ register and the candidate was referred on a hiring certificate.

At that point, apart from the candidate's score or ranking in the register, the hiring agency was most interested in a compelling resume and the candidate's listing of cases.

OPM specified the case listing format as follows:

1. Title of case
2. Party represented
3. Regulatory body or court hearing the case
4. Brief statement of issue(s) involved
5. Your precise role or capacity
6. Final disposition of case
7. Dates between which your participation took place
8. Presiding officer/judge with contact information (i.e., name, title/position, email address [if possible], and phone number)
9. Opposing counsel (or counsel appearing in case if applicant served in a hearing officer/judicial position) with contact information (i.e., name, title/position, email address [if possible], and phone number)

A representative sample is provided below.

Sample Case Listing – ALJ Candidate JOHN SMITH

A.
1. **Anna Hunter v. Michael Astrue, Commissioner of Social Security Administration.**
2. Plaintiff.
3. United States District Court, Central District of California.
4. Wrongful denial of benefits case, involving post-traumatic stress disorder in a surgical nurse.
5. Represented plaintiff throughout case.
6. Case was remanded for further proceedings, and plaintiff was ultimately awarded benefits.
7. 1/21/2011–12/18/2012.
8. Paul L. Abrams, United States Magistrate Judge, 312 North Spring Street, Room G, 9th Floor Los Angeles, CA 90012-4701, 213.894.7103.
9. Johnny King, Special Assistant United States Attorney, Social Security Administration, 333 Market St., Suite 1500 San Francisco, CA 94105, 123.456.7890, Johnny.King@ssa.gov.

B.
1. **Belinda Ganuba v. JoAnne B. Barnhart, Commissioner of Social Security Administration.**
2. Plaintiff.
3. United States District Court, District of Hawaii.
4. Wrongful denial of benefits case, involving complex facts, a voluminous record, and a disability ultimately tied to Lyme disease.
5. Represented plaintiff throughout case.
6. Case was remanded for further proceedings, and plaintiff was ultimately awarded benefits.
7. 11/3/2010–5/9/2011.
8. Leslie E. Kobayashi, United States Magistrate Judge, 300 Ala Moana Blvd., Honolulu, Hawaii 96850, 808.541.1331.
9. Frederico Lang, Assistant United States Attorney, PJKK Federal Building, 300 Ala Moana Boulevard, Room 6-100, Honolulu, Hawaii 96850, 234.567.8901.

C.
1. **Wichita Lineman v. Jo Anne B. Barnhart, Commissioner of Social Security Administration.**
2. Plaintiff.
3. United States District Court, Eastern District of Michigan.
4. Wrongful denial of benefits case, involving a closed head injury in a telephone technician who sustained an on the job injury following a fall, for which workers compensation benefits had been denied after lengthy proceedings.
5. Represented plaintiff throughout case.
6. Case was remanded for further proceedings, and plaintiff was ultimately awarded benefits.
7. 1/2/2009–6/27/2010.
8. Bernard A. Friedman, United States District Court Judge, Theodore Levin U.S.
9. Courthouse, 231 W. Lafayette Blvd., Room 101 Detroit, MI 48226, 313.234.5170.
10. Glenda Campbell, Assistant United States Attorney, 101 First Street, Suite 200, Bay City, MI 48708-5747, 989.123.4567, glenda.campbell@usdoj.gov.

ALJ APPLICATION AND TEST PROCEDURES

PART 2 - COMPETITIVE APPLICATION

A. The 13 ALJ Competencies

In 2013, applicants who cleared the qualifications screening were next required to participate in multi-part online testing. This consisted of a Situational Judgment Test (SJT), which was avatar-driven, an online Writing Sample (WR), and a multiple choice Experience Assessment (EA). The highest-scoring applicants, based on those who completed the online testing, were next invited to participate in an onsite, proctored exam. This included a Written Demonstration (WD) and a Logic-Based Measurement Test (LBMT). This was followed, on the next day, by a Structured Interview.

This was a much more complicated process than that employed in 2009, although in 2009, the application process itself was much more onerous. The purpose of the new, multi-phase process was to better evaluate applicants' competencies (knowledge, skills, and abilities), essential to choosing high-quality, hard-working ALJs who would be accountable for producing high volumes of quality decisions, principally at the Social Security Administration.

Six (6) competencies were evaluated in the 2009 ALJ exam. The 2013 announcement expanded this list to thirteen (13):

- ✦ Decision Making*
- ✦ Interpersonal Skills*
- ✦ Judicial Analysis*
- ✦ Judicial Decisiveness
- ✦ Judicial Management*
- ✦ Judicial Temperament
- ✦ Litigation and Courtroom Competence
- ✦ Oral Communication*

- ✦ Problem Solving
- ✦ Professionalism
- ✦ Reasoning
- ✦ Self-Management
- ✦ Writing*

*Included and defined in 2009

The 2009 announcement expressly defined the six (6) competencies, and required accomplishment narratives dedicated to each of them as part of the application process. In contrast, the 2013 ALJ announcement failed to define any of the competencies, and narratives addressing them were not required, at least not as part of the initial application.

No one can predict with certainty what form the 2016 ALJ announcement will take. Nevertheless, it is worth studying these competencies and reflecting upon one's specific accomplishments and experiences—ones that are probative of the candidate's potential to perform well as an ALJ.

As an actual candidate, beyond merely thinking about these competencies, take time to write down your recent, relevant career achievements and pro bono accomplishments. In what manner are they probative of your own propensity to perform well as an ALJ? These written examples may be used to

- ✦ Craft accomplishment summaries for your ALJ resume;

- ✦ Prepare accomplishment narratives in preparation for an online exam;

- ✦ Draft accomplishment narratives for extended competency writing if required in the 2016 announcement; and/or

- ✦ Prepare accomplishment stories for your Structured Interview.

For each example, provide a general statement of the situation or circumstances (Challenge/Legal Context). Describe exactly what you did, including how you addressed challenging aspects of the situation or problem (Actions). Finally, describe the outcome (Results). Applicable to nearly all civilian agencies' hiring and performance evaluation processes, across the Federal government, this is known as "CCAR" or accomplishment writing. On the Resume Place website, at http://www.resume-place.com/resources/ccar-builder/, you will find a tool that facilitates accomplishment writing using the CCAR format. Under the "Results" category, make sure to include client outcomes as well as institutional or organizational outcomes.

Here is an example:

ALJ Competency: Problem Solving

Summary: Successfully defended Board of County Commissioners in highly sensitive, public, and complex lawsuit from the County Convention and Visitors Bureau and successfully organized effort for a new Bureau to serve the county's tourism industry.

Challenge/Context: In 2008, the County Convention and Visitors Bureau (CVB), which had been operating with public tax dollars, sued Clarkson County. The case attracted public attention, with many articles appearing in the local newspaper. CVB sought a writ of mandamus ordering County Commissioners to collect a hotel bed tax and turn the money over to them. The CVB also sought damages for breach of contract, amounting to $350K+ per year in unpaid tax collections. At the time, I was serving as a County Attorney, representing the Board of County Commissioners.

Actions: I successfully defended this lawsuit in an extremely high profile and sensitive context. I managed my clients' expectations, addressed the media aspects by cautioning my clients appropriately and preparing carefully crafted written statements for release. Through written and oral discovery, as well as careful review and analysis of written records, and substantial legal research, I was able to craft a compelling motion for summary judgment, which the plaintiffs were hard pressed to oppose. I made a successful oral argument when this motion was heard, following which the court informed plaintiffs that their case was without merit. To bring the case to a successful conclusion without placing county funds at unnecessary risk, and in a manner that was consistent with the public interest, I then negotiated a settlement in which nearly $200K in public tax money would be distributed to relevant tourism entities.

The CVB disbanded because it was out of money. I then organized the effort to replace the disbanded CVB. To better serve the community, I partnered with private sector community leaders to develop plans for a new CVB that addressed many of the issues that had given rise to the litigation. With my clients' permission and with the collaboration of private sector community leaders, I drafted the by-laws for a new private corporation.

Results: The new County Tourism Bureau is in its fifth year of operation. This membership-based organization has 200+ members.

Obviously, this story addresses multiple competencies, not just the one identified (Problem Solving). Which others do you see?

Candidates' stories often address more than one competency. Try to prepare as many examples as you need to ensure you are able to address all of the competencies listed in the 2013 announcement. Relevant definitions, and their sources, are also provided below:

Competency 1. Decision Making (definition from 2009 ALJ announcement): Makes sound, well-informed, objective, and timely decisions; perceives the impact and implications of decisions; commits to action, even in uncertain situations, to accomplish goals.

Competency 2. Interpersonal Skills (definition from 2009 ALJ announcement): Shows understanding, friendliness, courtesy, tact, empathy, concern, and politeness to others; develops and maintains effective relationships with others; deals effectively with individuals who are difficult, assertive, hostile, or distressed; relates well to people from varied backgrounds and different situations; is sensitive to cultural diversity, race, gender, disabilities, and other differences.

Competency 3. Judicial Analysis (definition from 2009 ALJ announcement): Analyzes, evaluates and weighs all evidence, including technical subject matter; defines issues and makes findings of fact and conclusions of law, which are appropriate to the case; articulates basis for the outcome.

Competency 4. Writing (definition from 2009 ALJ announcement): Recognizes and uses correct English grammar, punctuation, and spelling; communicates information (for example, facts, ideas, or messages) in writing in a succinct and organized manner; produces written information, which may include technical material, that is appropriate for the intended audience.

Competency 5. Judicial Management (definition from 2009 ALJ announcement): Knows and applies legal, trial, and evidentiary rules and procedures; presides at, participates in, and/or facilitates conferences, hearings, and meetings with sensitivity, diplomacy and impartiality; develops a full and fair record (for example, elicits facts, when appropriate, by examining lay and expert witnesses and by other means); gives all sides a fair opportunity to be heard; works with others to find mutually acceptable solutions.

Competency 6. Oral Communication (definition from 2009 ALJ announcement): Expresses information (for example, conclusions, rationale, ideas or facts) to individuals or groups effectively, taking into account the audience and nature of the information (for example, technical, sensitive, controversial); makes clear and convincing oral presentations; listens to others, attends to nonverbal cues, and responds appropriately.

Competency 7. Judicial Decisiveness (definition from American Judicature Society, Handbook for Judicial Nominating Commissioners, 2nd Edition, Ch. 5: Evaluative Criteria[1]): A trial judge in particular must be capable of making quick decisions under pressure. Often a trial judge will be required to rule on objections as soon as they are raised. Motions, too, will require prompt decisions if cases are to progress. A trial judge must be able to keep cases moving and be willing and able to reach decisions. He or she must be able to quickly assimilate law and facts and to respond to issues raised by counsel with confidence and without hesitation. The judge must be willing to make hard decisions and be able to rule with firmness. An appellate judge also must act decisively to draft and circulate arguments in support of, or in dissent to, draft opinions in order to facilitate the appellate decision-making process.

Competency 8. Judicial Temperament (definition from American Judicature Society Handbook for Judicial Nominating Commissioners, 2nd Edition, Ch. 5: Evaluative Criteria): Judicial temperament encompasses a variety of noble qualities. One of these qualities is dignity. To be dignified a judge must possess "quiet, tactful ways, and calm yet firm assurance." A jurist with appropriate judicial temperament uses authority gracefully. Judicial temperament also requires sensitivity and understanding. An understanding judge is sensitive to the feelings of those before the court, recognizing that each and every case is important to the participants. Finally, a candidate is not

---

1 http://www.judicialselection.us/uploads/documents/JNC_HandbkCh5_1185464391875.pdf.

temperamentally suited for the bench unless he or she possesses great patience. Patience is simply the ability to be even-tempered and to exercise restraint in trying situations.

Alternative definition from Standards on State Judicial Selection, ABA Standing Committee on Judicial Independence, July 2000, Paragraph iv[2]: Judicial temperament includes a commitment to equal justice under law, freedom from bias, ability to decide issues according to law, courtesy and civility, open-mindedness and compassion.

Competency 9. Litigation and Courtroom Competence (comparable to definition of "professional competence" from Standards on State Judicial Selection, ABA Standing Committee on Judicial Independence, July 2000, Paragraph iii): Professional competence includes intellectual capacity, professional and personal judgment, writing and analytical ability, knowledge of the law and breadth of professional experience, including courtroom and trial experience. Candidates for appellate judgeships should further demonstrate scholarly writing and academic talent, and the ability to write to develop a coherent body of law.

Competency 10. Problem Solving (definition from OPM's MOSAIC Competencies: Professional & Administrative Occupations 1996-1997[3]): Identifies problems; determines accuracy and relevance of information; uses sound judgment to generate and evaluate alternatives, and to make recommendations.

Competency 11. Professionalism (comparable to definition of "integrity" from American Judicature Society Handbook for Judicial Nominating Commissioners, 2nd Edition, Ch. 5: Evaluative Criteria[4]): This is another touchstone criterion. The responsibility of judges to make decisions that affect lives and fortunes requires the selection of men and women of unquestioned integrity. At a minimum, integrity means intellectual honesty, moral vigor and professional uprightness. It also requires a sense of honor, trustworthiness and absolute sincerity and reliability. A judge with integrity is unswervingly ethical. Ethical conduct by judges requires, at a minimum, commitment and adherence to the law, the Code of Judicial Conduct and the Code of Professional Responsibility.[5]

Competency 12. Reasoning (definition from OPM's MOSAIC Competencies: Professional & Administrative Occupations, 1996-1997[6]): Identifies rules, principles, or relationships that explain facts, data, or other information; analyzes information and makes correct inferences or draws accurate conclusions.

Competency 13. Self-Management (definition from OPM's MOSAIC Competencies: Professional & Administrative Occupations, 1996-1997[7]): Sets well-defined and realistic personal goals; displays a high level of initiative, effort, and commitment towards completing assignments in a timely manner; works with minimal supervision; is motivated to achieve; demonstrates responsible behavior.

---

2 http://www.americanbar.org/content/dam/aba/administrative/judicial_independence/reformat.authcheckdam.pdf.

3 http://www.opm.gov/policy-data-oversight/assessment-and-selection/competencies/mosaic-study-competencies-master-list.pdf.

4 http://www.opm.gov/policy-data-oversight/assessment-and-selection/competencies/mosaic-study-competencies-master-list.pdf.

5 To alert candidates to the ethical standards to which judges must adhere, a number of nominating commissions send aspiring judges a copy of their Code of Judicial Conduct along with the applicant questionnaire.

6 See note 4.

7 *Ibid.*

Among all of the competencies, "Judicial Temperament" is the hardest to pin down. If OPM hasn't defined this term for ALJ candidates, how do we know what it is?

Although the American Bar Association Standing Committee on the Federal Judiciary evaluates the professional qualifications of nominees to the Federal courts, which covers Article III judges but not ALJs, its views are nevertheless valuable. The ABA measures judicial temperament based on a nominee's compassion, decisiveness, open-mindedness, courtesy, patience, freedom from bias, and commitment to equal justice under the law.

In his 2007 book, *The Supreme Court: The Personalities and Rivalries That Defined America*, noted author and legal commentator Jeffrey Rosen quotes Supreme Court Chief Justice John Roberts:

> *I think judicial temperament is a willingness to step back from your own committed views of the correct jurisprudential approach and evaluate those views in terms of your role as a judge.... It's the difference between being a judge and being a law professor, and appreciating that it's not so much a question of analytical coherence or overview, it's more a question of where this fits in with the Court's established body of law. And how it's going to be received as law.*

Rosen opines that judicial temperament requires a judge to step away from personal ideologies and "factor in the Court's institutional role" in the interests of consensus and stability.

Whether preparing content for inclusion in the resume, drafting practice narratives in preparation for writing one or more accomplishment stories as may be required as part of the 2016 ALJ examination process, or developing CCARs as competency talking points in preparation for the Structured Interview, an ALJ candidate must be ready to prove his or her worth. The ability to tell stories that reflect one's readiness to become an ALJ is paramount.

All candidates should think carefully about the career accomplishments and experiences that have prepared them to take on the adjudicative responsibilities of an ALJ, not only with respect to the law and the parties before them, but also in terms of institutional stewardship.

Note from the Authors: The Resume Place offers consulting services, resume writing, and other one-on-one support for ALJ candidates. This includes resume writing, an assessment of litigation experience and career accomplishments most likely to reflect that the candidate has met the required qualifications/competencies, accomplishment writing, and preparation for Structured Interviews, to include recorded mock interviews. (We provide this service to senior level candidates across the Federal government—often as a Federal government contractor hired by the agencies themselves to support their top performers' career advancement.) Like preparing for the bar exam by taking a bar review course, or getting help with a resume to apply for any Federal job, this is *not* considered cheating.

B. Online Testing

In 2013, the invitation to participate in online testing was issued only after the ALJ candidate's qualifications were reviewed by OPM's Human Resources personnel, who required precise adherence to every requirement set forth in the application process. Applicants were rejected for failing to meet the minimum qualifications if, for example, they failed to include their bar number or failed to specify, in their qualifications narratives, the inclusive month and year reflecting their litigation and/ or administrative law experience, even if the period identified clearly reflected decades of full-time qualifying experience.[1]

In 2013, the online testing consisted of a Situational Judgment Test (SJT), an Experience Assessment (EA) and a Writing Sample (WS). Final numerical ratings were not issued until the assessment and examination process was completed for all applicants.[2]

The Situational Judgment Test (SJT)

The 2013 ALJ exam was the first to administer an avatar-driven SJT. Although candidates were not able to access the SJT until a specific 13-day window opened, a virtual sample was provided. This sample revealed that the SJT would be used to assess six (6) of the thirteen (13) competencies: decision making, interpersonal skills, judicial management, judicial temperament, litigation and courtroom competence, and problem solving. (Note: some but not all of these six competencies required an accomplishment narrative in 2009.)

The SJT presented a set of work-related problems and decision-making situations. Applicants were required to choose which of the multiple-choice responses they would most likely or least likely take. The SJT was timed, and involved both text-based scenarios and video-based scenarios with closed captioning. Applicants could review the instructions as long as they wished, but were given only 75 minutes to respond to the questions.

Although it is not possible to know the precise questions OPM will ask, it can be helpful to refer to this page for more information about situational judgment tests: http://www.opm.gov/policy-data-oversight/assessment-and-selection/other-assessment-methods/situational-judgment-tests/.

---

1 Others were excluded for technical reasons, such as difficulty navigating the application interface. This led to many appeals, some of which earned candidates a revised determination and an invitation to continue.

2 Not including those who applied outside of the open period, such as Schedule A applicants or 10-point veterans, who are allowed to apply to closed announcements. See Appendix B.

The Experience Assessment (EA)

The EA consisted of multiple-choice and open-ended questions about work experience related to ALJ positions. Applicants were required to select among multiple-choice responses and write a narrative response, if requested, consistent with their experience associated with the targeted competency. The EA was not timed. Unfortunately, there was no OPM preview, and applicants were precluded from copying the questions or sharing them with others.

If the EA requires candidates to characterize their level of experience in various areas, they should choose the highest level they can support with an example, if asked to do so. Federal hiring specialists typically compare a candidate's questionnaire answers with the record of activities reflected in the resume. This provides yet another reason to submit a polished Federal outline format resume, with key accomplishments relevant to the ALJ competencies summarized beneath each job description. Also, if the questionnaire includes a text box requiring candidates to elaborate upon their answer, candidates should be prepared to supply a succinct CCAR narrative in support of the claimed competency. Again, preparing a selection of examples in advance that speak to the 13 competencies could prove very helpful.

The Writing Sample (WS)

The 2013 exam was also the first to include a timed, online writing exercise. Non-applicants were not able to view the WS and candidates were not permitted to share its content with others. Applicants could take as long as they wanted to review the instructions but were given 35 minutes to prepare a narrative response to the question. However, candidates could log out of the system to work on their answers and log back in to type it online. While logged out, the clock would stop, enabling applicants to prepare a response offline and then log back in to type their essay online. Pasting prewritten content was not possible, as the exact question(s) were a surprise.

However, the 2013 ALJ exam experience suggests candidates can benefit from practicing the writing of accomplishment narratives in advance of the online exam. These narratives are not meant for copy-pasting into the exam; merely, they give the candidate much-needed experience responding to accomplishment-based questions in a concise manner. Upon viewing the question, exit the system and prepare a response. Only after the response is completed, and spell checked, log back in and type the essay into the system.

To score highly, candidates across the Federal hiring landscape need to feel comfortable using the first-person storytelling structure most commonly associated with OPM evaluation and hiring processes—the CCAR. Past candidates have reported not only success using this process, but also a degree of confidence that enabled them to complete every phase of the process with the best information possible.

C. In-Person Examination and Structured Interview

If the 2016 ALJ announcement reveals a process similar to that employed in 2013, candidates will be notified of their selection to sit for a live, proctored exam only after all candidates complete the online exam and their scores are tallied. Indeed, in 2013, a few months after the online component was completed, those with the highest scores were invited to the designated testing location. Candidates first completed a two-part, proctored exam, and thereafter attended an in-person, structured interview.

In 2013, the proctored component included a Written Demonstration (WD) as well as a Logic-Based Measurement Test (LBMT). Later, additional groups of candidates were invited to sit for the two-part, proctored exam and participate in a structured interview. This included candidates whose appeals resulted in reappraisals of their applications and/or rescoring of their online exams, as well as candidates who received lower passing scores on the online exam.

The Written Demonstration (WD)

The WD is intended to evaluate the candidate's ability to prepare a clear, concise, and well-reasoned legal decision of the type one might write as an ALJ. In 2013, the WD was scheduled for five (5) hours to allow time for instructions and other administrative processes, but actual testing time was four (4) hours. It was conducted in a proctored environment, and candidates used a laptop computer provided by OPM. Candidates who failed to achieve a required minimum score did not receive a final numerical rating and were not placed on the ALJ register. The WD was based on fictitious laws, so there was no point in trying to study "law" for it.

If administrative decision writing is new to you, you may benefit from studying some decisions written by real ALJs and consulting texts such as the *Writing Deskbook for Administrative Law Judges: An Introduction*, by Michael H. Frost & Paul A. Bateman (Carolina Academic Press, 2010), and the *Manual for Administrative Law Judges*, by Professor Morell E. Mullins, at http://digitalcommons. pepperdine.edu/naalj/vol23/iss3/1 (published by the National Association of Administrative Law Judiciary in collaboration with Pepperdine University). The ALJ Manual is listed as one of the NAALJ's most popular papers.

Other ALJ manuals are available online or can be found by searching Google Books. The Administrative Law and Regulatory Practice Section of the ABA is also helpful. Its *Guide to Federal Agency Adjudication*, now in its second edition, by Jeffrey B. Litwak, is available for sale on ABA's website.

Finally, remember that the WD is much like a bar exam. You will take bathroom breaks on your own time, and should bring pens or pencils for taking notes and a snack and beverage to keep you going.

The Logic-Based Measurement Test (LBMT)

The LBMT provides a variety of scenarios with multiple-choice responses. Only one answer in each scenario is logically correct; the others are not. Applicants must choose one response. The LBMT is also conducted in a proctored environment. In 2013, the actual testing time was approximately two (2) hours, but candidates were allotted 2.5 hours to include time for instructions. All candidates were required to complete the WD and LBMT before participating in the Structured Interview.

As with other parts of the examination process, the questions used for the LBMT are a secret. However, it is possible to prepare for this type of testing. For example, you may want to review the sample questions provided to Special Agent candidates by the FBI: https://www.fbijobs.gov/sites/default/files/SpecialAgentPhaseISampleTest.pdf, pages 2–4.

Also, review the preparation manual used to familiarize U.S. Immigration and Customs Enforcement agents for testing. ICE (and other Federal law enforcement employers) test the same fact-finding skills that OPM will test aspiring ALJs for.

As ICE advises,

> *The questions in this examination are designed to test your ability to understand complicated written material and to derive correct conclusions from it. The kind of reading that these questions ask you to do is different from ordinary reading in which you just follow the general meaning of a series of sentences to see what the writer thinks about a topic. It is the kind of reading you have to do with complex material when you intend to take some action or draw some conclusion based on that material.*

Also:

> *In answering the questions, it is important that you accept every fact in the paragraph as true. Remember that you are not being judged on your knowledge of facts, but rather on your ability to read and reason on the basis of given facts.[1]*

---

1 http://www.ice.gov/doclib/careers/pdf/satestprep.pdf, page 5.

The Structured Interview (SI)

OPM does not reveal the specific questions included in the Administrative Law Judge SI. Candidates and interviewing panel members are sworn to secrecy. Despite the secrecy, much is known about the process that can help ALJ candidates prepare.

OPM itself designed the structured interview process for use across all of Federal civilian hiring; also, much insight is available based on how other agencies evaluate potential adjudicators. Past interview questions have been gleaned from OPM's non-ALJ interviews, the Social Security Administration's non-ALJ interviews, and other agencies' judicial candidate interviews, such as those for Administrative Patent Judges, Immigration Judges, and Administrative Judges (non-ALJs), generally.

The typical interview is both "performance based" and "behavioral." OPM describes the process and informs agencies how to conduct structured interviews in its own document, *Structured Interviews: A Practical Guide* (OPM 2008).[2] At the same time, it is actually the Department of Veterans Affairs which has the better website devoted to performance-based interviewing. As the VA describes,

> *Research findings show that the best predictor of future behavior is past behavior. The job-related questions help the interviewer better evaluate applicants fairly and improve the match between people and jobs. This method is also referred to as competency-based or behavioral interviewing.*[3]

All candidates are likely to be asked to tell the panel about themselves, why they should be selected as an ALJ, and why they want the job. In essence, candidates should be prepared to give a brief opening statement on their own behalves, summarizing their education, experience, and specialties and defining their top or unique accomplishments, consistent with the ALJ competencies. In responding to why the candidate wants the job, the answer should focus upon what motivates one to serve, not upon the prestige that an ALJ appointment will bring.

The ALJ structured interview has been described as "awkward," which confirms the assessment that it is of the now popular "behavioral" type. This means there will likely be several questions that take the following form:

> Can you give us an example of what you did to resolve a difficult, on-the-job conflict with others regarding how to address a case management problem?

Or:

> Can you tell us about a difficult client or litigant who was angry, upset, or intellectually challenged, and how you managed that relationship and resolved the situation?

---

2 https://www.opm.gov/policy-data-oversight/assessment-and-selection/structured-interviews/guide.pdf.
3 http://www.va.gov/pbi/.

In each case, interviewers are setting up the applicant to relate an accomplishment story in which the interviewee serves as the hero of his or her own story. These stories are all told in a specific way—using the CCAR. Within a few minutes, candidates should be able to orient the panelists in space and time (Context), identify the problem in all its complexity (Challenge), describe what the applicant personally did to resolve the situation (Actions), and conclude with the specific outcome attained, including any metrics (settlement values, periods of time, percentage improvement, etc.) (Results).

The CCAR can be used to develop thoughtful answers to hypothetical questions. For example:

Question: What would you do if you were hearing a case as an ALJ and an unrepresented (or pro se) litigant, while testifying, threatened to commit suicide when the hearing was over?

There is no one-size-fits-all answer to this question, and indeed, ALJs are not trained for this issue. A thoughtful ALJ candidate/interviewee might consider giving a response along the following lines:

Answer: Well, first I think I would want to know more about the circumstances. For example, how much do I know about this litigant? Does this individual have a mental health care provider and is that person's record of care part of this case? Is that person available or is there someone other than myself who can more appropriately provide a response in this situation? (Context/Challenge)

As to what I would do—first, I think I would find out if there is a specific policy that I am supposed to follow in situations like this. If there was nothing in writing, I might ask a more senior ALJ for assistance before resorting to my own devices. If all else failed, and if their mental health care provider was not immediately available to take charge of the situation, and if I felt this person was really making a direct threat to harm himself, rather than simply expressing frustration at the legal process, I would have my law clerk find one of the court-appointed mental health care experts if he or she was known to be onsite that day. Or else perhaps a sworn law enforcement officer, if one is onsite, to notify them of what has taken place. This law enforcement professional or the court-appointed mental health care professional would have specific procedures to follow and therefore would be much better able than I would be to take the right action in this setting. (Actions)

When all was said and done, I would expect this individual to be taken into an appropriate facility for an evaluation, or else a proper initial assessment to be made before the litigant leaves the building, with the litigant told what to do in terms of seeking help in the future. Also, if the litigant came back at a later time to testify, I would first inquire as to whether he or she was okay to proceed. I would hope that these actions resulted in a good outcome in terms of the litigant's health and safety, and also ensured the integrity of my decision-making process. (Results)

Because narrative responses are expected, not simple yes or no answers, candidates should wear a wristwatch and keep track of the time. The length of the interview will be disclosed in advance. It is appropriate to ask how many questions there will be, and then structure one's time so as to answer every question before the interview concludes. The interview may be scored, with unanswered questions scored as a "0."

While the candidate is answering, interviewers will remain stone faced and silent. There will be no chitchat. The structured interview is like a bad deposition. Questioners know all of the questions, and follow a script, but unlike a deposition, if the interviewee says something extremely interesting, the questioners will not follow up or otherwise go off script to delve deeper. Finally, silence will follow most answered questions. Candidates must resist the urge to begin talking again.

Once this part is over, based on past experience with the process, it could take anywhere from two to five months to learn one's final numerical score. Successful ALJ candidates then join the ALJ Register, and the selection process for Social Security's Office of Disability and Review commences thereafter.

CONCLUSION

A Review, Plus Some Parting Advice

Plan ahead. Prepare your application in advance, as best as you can. Understand the position description and the requisite skill set. Once the new ALJ job announcement is posted on USAJOBS, read it very carefully.

Meanwhile, set up your USAJOBS.gov account now. On February 7, 2013, OPM issued a press release announcing its intent to create a new ALJ register "in the near future." The ALJ announcement posted on March 5, 2013, and remained open for ten (10) days. Set up a saved search tailored for 0935 series jobs on USAJOBS.gov, using the advanced search feature. Have the system email search results to you on a daily basis.

When the announcement posts, familiarize yourself with the entire examination process, including the ways it is consistent with or may be different from past exams. Learn what is necessary for success at each stage: the Federal resume, the qualifying experience narratives, the nature and types of online and in-person testing, including any narrative writing and/or sample decision writing, and finally, the structured interview. Although the requirements for the AL-0935 job series remained the same from 2009 to 2013, the 2013 announcement and examination process was very different from that announced in 2009. In 2016, it could be different yet again.

Meanwhile:

✦ While you are waiting for the announcement to post, make a list of your top career accomplishments. Flesh out the best and most recent ones, using the CCAR structure. Make sure the narratives contain a context, a challenge, a description of your own actions, and the specific results you obtained. Include stories from community/pro bono service, organizational stewardship, and teaching/mentoring. Use this as your source material; it will be of use to you regardless of the form of the next ALJ announcement.

✦ Create your outline format Federal resume. Your outline format Federal resume should respond to the requirements of the position with respect to your lawyering and litigation skills, and should detail your substantive expertise. Use your top career accomplishment material to build out your resume, supplementing your relevant duties and responsibilities with specific accomplishments. Build your ALJ resume online on USAJOBS.gov, and also upload it to your account as a Word document.

✦ Document your qualifying experience for the Occupational Assessment narratives and make sure your resume is consistent with what you have described. Don't just claim you have seven (7) years of full-time qualifying litigation and/or administrative law experience: Describe it. Make it clear that your qualifying experience was full time. Provide examples. Use numbers.

✦ Prepare for the various types of testing described in this guide by studying relevant online examples from other Federal jobs. Before attending the written demonstration, study some sample ALJ decisions and practice writing them. There are excellent resources published online and elsewhere (some cited in this book) that can help you learn to write a good decision.

✦ Learn about structured/behavioral interviews. Although ALJ candidates are sworn to secrecy about their interviews, there is much you can do to prepare. If you make it this far, there are free materials online and coaches who can help you. At a minimum, review your top CCAR narratives and be prepared to tell a compelling story, in five minutes or less, that speaks to each of the relevant judicial skills.

In the past, it has taken perhaps another month or so before the first offers of employment were extended. All told, the time between applying and being offered a job has been nine (9) to ten (10) months. ALJs seeking jobs in agencies other than SSA must be on the lookout for them through USAJOBS.gov. Keep in mind that other agencies do hire ALJs away from SSA. Recognizing that the vast majority of ALJs are hired by SSA, many candidates interview with and accept offers from SSA, build up their credibility and experience as a disability judge, and then transfer to another agency when the right opportunity becomes available.

The 2013 ALJ Announcement

Search Jobs ❓

Where: ▶

Advanced Search >

< Back to Results

This Position Is No Longer Available

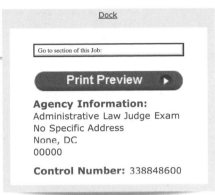

Dock

Go to section of this Job:

Print Preview ▶

Agency Information:
Administrative Law Judge Exam
No Specific Address
None, DC
00000

Control Number: 338848600

| Overview | Duties | Qualifications & Evaluations | Benefits & Other Info | How to Apply |

Multi-Agency

Job Title: Administrative Law Judge
Agency: Multi-agency
Job Announcement Number: ALJ2013-847661

SALARY RANGE:	$118,612.00 to $165,300.00 / Per Year
OPEN PERIOD:	Tuesday, March 05, 2013 to Friday, March 15, 2013
SERIES & GRADE:	AL-0935-03
POSITION INFORMATION:	Full Time - Permanent
DUTY LOCATIONS:	Many vacancies in the following location(s):
	Santa Barbara, CA United States View Map
	Denver, CO United States View Map
	Hartford, CT United States View Map
	Miami, FL United States View Map
	Tampa, FL United States View Map
	More Locations (174)
WHO MAY APPLY:	United States Citizens
JOB SUMMARY:	

Administrative Law Judges (ALJ) serve as independent impartial triers of fact in formal proceedings requiring a decision on the record after the opportunity for a hearing. In general, ALJs prepare for and preside at formal hearings required by statute to be held under or in accordance with provisions of the Administrative Procedure Act (APA), codified in relevant part, in sections 553-559 of title 5, United States Code (U.S.C.). ALJs rule on preliminary motions, conduct pre-hearing conferences, issue subpoenas, conduct hearings (which may include written and/or oral testimony and cross-examination), review briefs, and prepare and issue decisions, along with written findings of fact and conclusions of law.

The Federal Government employs ALJs in a number of agencies throughout the United States and Puerto Rico. Cases may involve Federal laws and regulations in such areas as admiralty, advertising, antitrust, banking, communications, energy, environmental protection, food and drugs, health and safety, housing, immigration, interstate commerce, international trade, labor management relations, securities and commodities markets, social security disability and other benefits claims, and transportation.

Individuals who wish to apply for a position as an ALJ with the Federal Government should read this ALJ Job Opportunity Announcement in its entirety before preparing an application. Applicants must meet all the qualifications requirements for an ALJ position as described in this announcement.

OPM reserves the right to verify information provided by the applicant during the examination process and through any part of the selection process. Information that cannot be verified may result in designating the applicant as "ineligible" or negating the score on a particular examination component, depending upon the information at issue.

KEY REQUIREMENTS

- U.S. Citizenship
- Subject to a background suitability investigation/determination
- Submit all supporting documents (see "How to Apply" section)
- Registered for Selective Service, if applicable (see www.sss.gov)

DUTIES: Back to top

ALJs:

- conduct formal hearings involving cases where all interested parties are given advance notice of the hearing; an opportunity to submit facts, arguments, offers of settlement or proposals of adjustment; and an opportunity to be accompanied, represented, and advised by counsel or other qualified representatives;
- rule on preliminary motions, conduct pre-hearing conferences, issue subpoenas, control hearings (which may include written and/or oral testimony and cross-examination), review briefs, and receive or exclude (for example, on the ground that it is irrelevant, immaterial, or unduly repetitious) any oral or documentary evidence proffered for consideration; and
- prepare and issue decisions (or initial or recommended decisions), along with written findings of fact and conclusions of law therein, upon consideration of the whole record, or those parts of it cited by a party and supported by and in accord with reliable, probative, and substantial evidence.

QUALIFICATIONS REQUIRED: Back to top

Preliminary Qualifications:

As part of the qualifications requirements for an ALJ position, an applicant must meet all three of the following requirements:

1. Possess a full seven (7) years of experience as a licensed attorney preparing for, participating in, and/or reviewing formal hearings or trials involving litigation and/or administrative law at the Federal, State or local level;

2. Possess a professional license and be authorized to practice law under the laws of a State, the District of Columbia, the Commonwealth of Puerto Rico, or any territorial court established under the United States Constitution (see specific details regarding LICENSURE below);

3. Pass the U.S. Office of Personnel Management (OPM) competitive examination which evaluates the competencies, or knowledge, skills, and abilities, essential to performing the work of an ALJ.

Specific details for each of the three requirements above are as follows:

1. EXPERIENCE:

QUALIFYING EXPERIENCE: Applicants must have a full seven (7) years of experience as a licensed attorney preparing for, participating in, and/or reviewing formal hearings or trials involving litigation and/or administrative law at the Federal, State or local level. To be considered as qualifying experience, the types of cases handled under this requirement must have been conducted on the record under procedures at least as formal as those prescribed by sections 553 through 559 of title 5 of the United States Code.

Litigation Experience: Qualifying litigation experience involves cases in which a complaint was filed with a court, or a charging document (e.g., indictment or information) was issued by a court, a grand jury, or appropriate military authority and includes:

- participating in settlement or plea negotiations in advance of trial;
- preparing for trial and/or participating in trial of cases;
- preparing opinions;
- hearing cases;
- participating in or conducting arbitration, mediation, or other alternative dispute resolution process

Applicants who have cleared the preliminary qualifications screening (i.e., the experience and licensure requirements) also are required to successfully complete other components of the ALJ examination. The purpose of these remaining components is to evaluate the competencies, or knowledge, skills, and abilities, essential to performing the work of an ALJ. These competencies include: Decision Making, Interpersonal Skills, Judicial Analysis, Judicial Decisiveness, Judicial Management, Judicial Temperament, Litigation and Courtroom Competence, Oral Communication, Problem Solving, Professionalism, Reasoning, Self-Management, and Writing.

The remaining assessment components of the examination for ALJ positions are listed below and further described in the section **How You will be Evaluated, Basis for Rating:**

Online Component:
    Section 1 - Situational Judgment Test (SJT)
    Section 2 - Writing Sample
    Section 3 – Experience Assessment

Proctored Component:
    Section 1 – Written Demonstration (WD)
    Section 2 – Logic-Based Measurement Test (LBMT)

In-person Component:
    Structured Interview (SI)

HOW YOU WILL BE EVALUATED:

Basis for Rating:

After you submit a complete online Application Package and you have cleared the preliminary qualifications screening, you will receive information and an internet link via email concerning an upcoming time period in which you must complete the Situational Judgment Test (SJT), Writing Sample, and Experience Assessment online. If you do not complete the SJT, Writing Sample, and Experience Assessment in the required time period, a Notice of Results (NOR) will be issued to you indicating a rating of "ineligible" and no further action will be taken on your application.

Online Component: Situational Judgment Test (SJT), Writing Sample, and Experience Assessment

Section 1: SJT - The SJT presents applicants with a set of work-related problems or critical situations and asks applicants to indicate which of the multiple-choice response options they would most likely and least likely take to handle the situations. The SJT is administered online, is timed, and involves text-based scenarios as well as video-based scenarios with closed captioning. Applicants may take as long as they wish to review the instructions but are given 75 minutes to respond to the SJT questions.

Section 2: Writing Sample - The Writing Sample is an exercise in which applicants write a response to a pre-determined topic. Applicants type their writing sample responses online and the exercise is timed. Applicants may take as long as they wish to review the instructions but are given 35 minutes to prepare a response to the question.

Section 3: Experience Assessment - The Experience Assessment includes multiple-choice and open-ended questions about work experience that is related to ALJ positions. Applicants select a multiple-choice response and write a narrative response, as appropriate, to indicate and document their experience associated with the targeted competency. The Experience Assessment is not timed.

Applicants who are invited to participate in the SJT, Writing Sample, and Experience Assessment will receive an advance email with specific instructions for completing these assessments and details about computer system requirements. Once you have submitted your responses to the online assessments (i.e., SJT, Writing Sample, and Experience Assessment), you will not be allowed to make changes to your submission.

If the score for your performance on the SJT, Writing Sample, and Experience Assessment is within the range for the higher-scored sub-group of all the eligible applicants, you will be invited to participate in the Written Demonstration and Logic-Based Measurement Test, and the Structured Interview. You will be notified via email regarding when and where to report for the Written Demonstration and Logic-Based Measurement Test, and for the Structured Interview.

If the score for your performance on the SJT, Writing Sample, and Experience Assessment is not within the range for the higher-scored sub-group of eligible applicants, you will be notified via email that you will no longer be considered for this current ALJ Job Opportunity Announcement. You will not be invited to participate in the Written Demonstration and Logic-Based Measurement Test or the Structured Interview. Your official Notice of Results and a notice describing your appeal rights will be issued after the U.S. Office of Personnel Management completes the administration of the ALJ examination for the entire group that participated in the examination.

NOTE: In determining the SJT, Writing Sample, and Experience Assessment score, veterans' preference points will be applied for applicants who are entitled to such points and have submitted the required documentation. For candidates who successfully complete the remaining components of the examination, preference points will then be withdrawn from the SJT, Writing Sample, and Experience Assessment score, so that veterans' preference points, when applied to the applicant's final score for the entire examination, will be counted only once.

Proctored Component: Written Demonstration (WD) and Logic-Based Measurement Test (LBMT). If you are invited to participate in the WD and LBMT, this component of the examination will be administered to you in one day in two separate sessions in a proctored environment.

Section 1: WD - The purpose of the WD is to evaluate an applicant's ability to prepare a clear, concise, and well-reasoned legal decision of the type that one might be expected to write if employed as an ALJ. The WD is scheduled for 5 hours to allow time for instructions and other administrative processes, but actual testing time is 4 hours. The WD is conducted in a proctored environment using a laptop computer provided by OPM, and will be administered in one location in the Washington, DC area.

If you do not receive the required minimum score on the WD, you will not receive a final numerical rating and will not be placed on the ALJ register.

Section 2: LBMT - The LBMT presents applicants with a set of scenarios and multiple-choice response options. Only one response option in each scenario is logically accurate, while the remaining options are logically inaccurate. Applicants are asked to indicate which one response option is logically accurate. The LBMT is conducted in a proctored environment and will be scheduled for 2½ hours to allow time for instructions, but actual testing time is approximately 2 hours. The LBMT will be administered in one location in the Washington, DC area.

You must complete the WD and LBMT before participating in the Structured Interview.

In-person Component: Structured Interview (SI). If you are invited to participate in the SI, this part of the examination will be administered in an in-person panel interview environment.

SI - The objective of the SI is to evaluate an applicant's responses to competency-based questions related to being an ALJ. A panel will conduct the interview and evaluate the responses provided by the applicant. The interview will last approximately one hour, but you will need to arrive early to allow time for instructions. The SI will be administered in one location in the Washington, DC area.

If you do not receive the required minimum score on the SI, you will not receive a final numerical rating and will not be placed on the ALJ register.

Final Numerical Rating: Applicants who complete all portions of the assessment process and achieve a minimum required score on both the WD and SI will be issued a final numerical rating on a scale of **1 – 100**. The rating will be based on the scores assigned for the SJT/Writing Sample/Experience Assessment, WD/LBMT, and SI components of the examination with a maximum possible total score of **100**, excluding veterans' preference. If you do not claim veterans' preference, this earned rating will be your final numerical rating. If you claim veterans' preference (other than on the basis of sole survivorship, as described below) and have submitted the required documentation, 5 or 10 points, as appropriate, will be added to your total earned rating to determine your final numerical rating.

Appeals Process: An ALJ Appeals Panel (Panel) will be convened to adjudicate any appeals after all final numerical ratings have been assigned to all applicants who applied during this ALJ Job Opportunity Announcement open period. The Panel will accept and adjudicate an appeal from the following four categories of applicants who believe their ratings were assigned in error:

1. An applicant who received a NOR indicating "ineligible" at any stage of the ALJ assessment process.

2. An applicant who received a NOR indicating that his/her SJT, Writing Sample, and Experience Assessment score was not within the range for the higher-scored sub-group of all the eligible applicants and therefore did not receive further consideration for this current ALJ Job Opportunity Announcement.

3. An applicant who did not receive a minimum required score on the WD and/or SI, did not receive a final numerical rating, and was not placed on the ALJ register.

4. An applicant who received a NOR with a final numerical rating, for appeal of the entire examination.

The Panel has the authority to **affirm, raise,** or **lower** the rating; change a rating from eligible to ineligible and **remove** an applicant from the register; or **remand** for further development. An appeal must be filed by email within 30 calendar days from the date of the NOR. Appeals are adjudicated based on the record. The decision of the Appeals Panel is final, and exhausts further administrative appeal rights. Additional details regarding the appeal process will be provided once the NOR has been issued.

NOTE: If you receive a final numerical rating, and your name is placed on the register, and you appeal your numerical rating, your name will remain on the register, associated with your original score of record while the appeal is being processed. If, however, you are selected for an ALJ position, your name will be removed from the register and your pending appeal cancelled.

Retaking the ALJ Examination: You may retake the ALJ examination when the examination is open to the receipt of new applications if:

- You did not pass the preliminary qualifications screening, or did not receive a minimum required score on the WD or SI;

- Your score was not within the range of the higher-scored sub-group of all eligible applicants for SJT, Writing Sample, and Experience Assessment; or

- You received a NOR with a final numerical rating and one year has passed since the date of the final NOR.

In any of the above situations, you will be bound by the result of retaking the examination. Please note that once you start retaking the examination, in order to receive a new final numerical rating and remain on the register, you must successfully complete all components of the examination. Your most recent rating will become your new rating of record, but this new rating can be higher than, the same as, or lower than the score you received previously, or it can be an ineligible rating.

NOTE: If you reapply for the examination while you have an appeal pending, the reapplication will automatically terminate the appeal.

If you are a 10-point veterans' preference eligible, you have the right to reopen the ALJ Job Opportunity Announcement at any time after it closes pursuant to 5 CFR 332.311, in order to participate in a quarterly examination. You have this right even if you have received a final numerical rating and your name has been placed on the register. You will, however, be bound by the result of retaking the examination. In other words, once you start retaking the examination, in order to receive a new final numerical rating and remain on the register, you must successfully complete all components of the examination. Your most recent rating will become your new rating of record, but this new rating can be higher than, the same as, or lower than the score you received previously, or it can be an ineligible rating.

Receiving Employment Consideration:

If you receive a NOR with a final numerical rating, your name will be placed on the new ALJ register. The ALJ register is a list of candidates eligible for selection used to make referrals to agencies for employment consideration when they have entry level ALJ vacancies to fill. Names are referred in descending rank order, based on the duty location of the position(s) to be filled and the geographical preference of candidates. It is the responsibility of the hiring agency to make selections from the list of candidates referred for employment consideration from among the highest three available names, taking into consideration veterans' preference and other civil service rules.

By submitting an ALJ application, you are expressing your interest and availability for ALJ employment.

- Declination of Job Offers: If you decline two (2) job offers you will be suspended from the ALJ register for a period of one (1) year or until the register is terminated, whichever comes first. If after one (1) year you wish to have your name returned to the ALJ register, you must submit your request in writing to the ALJ email address at: aljapplication@opm.gov. Your request to end your suspension and have your name returned to the register will be accepted as long as the register on which you were placed has not been terminated, and you continue to satisfy the licensure requirement.

- Non-Availability or Declination of Employment Consideration: As stated in the Geographic Availability section (see below), *"If after selecting your geographical location(s) you decline consideration for a geographical location(s) for which you indicated availability, you will be removed from further consideration for that location(s). You will not be able to reinstate a location from which you have been removed until the next ALJ Job Opportunity Announcement open period."* If you decline to be considered for any location(s) for which an agency is, at that time, seeking to consider you, you will be removed from further consideration for the location(s). Again, you will not be able to reinstate the location(s) until the next ALJ Job Opportunity Announcement filing period.

If you become unavailable for consideration for a period of time, you should request to have your name suspended due to unavailability from the register. Such requests for suspension, as well as requests to have your name restored to the register, must be submitted to aljapplication@opm.gov. Requests to end the suspension due to unavailability and have your name restored to the register will be accepted as long as the register on which you were placed has not been terminated, and you continue to satisfy the licensure requirement. The ALJ register is scheduled to expire in October 2015, although OPM may extend that date. Prior to the expiration date, applicants on the register will be notified regarding their status and any action impacting their eligibility.

If your name is referred for consideration from the register, and you fail to respond to an inquiry from the prospective employing agency, you will be considered unavailable for appointment, and your name will be suspended due to unavailability from the ALJ register until you request to have your name restored to the register as described in the preceding paragraph.

Note: It is important to notify OPM about your availability and changes to your contact information during the examination process and while you are on the register. OPM is not responsible for an applicant's non-receipt of official notifications due to outdated or inaccurate contact information concerning the applicant (i.e., email address), spam blockers or other email filters.

BENEFITS:
Back to top

The Federal Government offers a comprehensive benefits package. Explore the major benefits offered to most Federal employees at: https://help.usajobs.gov/index.php/Pay_and_Benefits.

OTHER INFORMATION:

HOW TO APPLY:
Back to top

To apply for the position of ALJ, you **must** submit the minimum complete application package through the online processing system (Application Manager). A minimum complete package includes the following:

1. Your responses to the Assessment Questionnaire, and
2. Your résumé as specified in the Required Documents section of this ALJ Job Opportunity Announcement.
3. Veterans' Preference documentation (if you are claiming Veterans' Preference).

In addition to these requirements, you may submit a listing of significant cases as described below. This is an **optional** document which can be uploaded in the "Other" document type.

LISTING OF SIGNIFICANT LITIGATION AND/OR ADMINISTRATIVE LAW CASES (OPTIONAL):
The case listing is optional. You may provide this information in support of your application by identifying specific examples of qualifying experience. You may use the case listing format provided below to cite and discuss **up to six (6) of the most significant** litigation and/or formal administrative law cases you have prepared, participated in, and/or reviewed.

The case listing document should be uploaded as a separate document in the "Other" document type of your application. The cases will not be scored as part of the ALJ examination but may be used by hiring agencies in their selection process. The cases will be provided to hiring agencies with your résumé if your name is on the new ALJ register and is referred on a hiring certificate.

The case listing format is as follows:

1. Title of case
2. Party represented
3. Regulatory body or court hearing the case
4. Brief statement of issue(s) involved
5. Your precise role or capacity
6. Final disposition of case
7. Dates between which your participation took place
8. Presiding officer/judge with contact information (i.e., name, title/position, email address (if possible), and phone number)
9. Opposing counsel (or counsel appearing in case if applicant served in a hearing officer/judicial position) with contact information (i.e., name, title/position, email address (if possible), and phone number)

Reasonable Accommodation for online ALJ Application: OPM provides reasonable accommodation to applicants with disabilities, where appropriate. Determinations on requests for accommodation(s) for the submission of the online application will be made on a case-by-case basis and must be requested before the close of the ALJ Job Opportunity Announcement. If you wish to request an accommodation(s) for the submission of the online application based on your disability, you must contact OPM for assistance by sending an email message to aljapplication@opm.gov.

Please note the following:

- Changes to assessment items in the Assessment Questionnaire or to your résumé or your list of significant cases will not be accepted after the ALJ Job Opportunity Announcement closes, although changes to non-assessment items (such as contact information) can be made by sending an email with the updated information to aljapplication@opm.gov.
- An application is considered complete when the Assessment Questionnaire and résumé (described in the "How to Apply" section) are submitted **and** the online SJT, Writing Sample, and Experience Assessment (described in the "Competitive Examination" section) have been completed within the designated timeframe.
- Failure to submit a complete application package, including failure to complete the SJT, Writing Sample, and Experience Assessment within the set timeframe, will cause your application to be rated "ineligible" and you will not be able to participate in the remaining components of the ALJ examination.

The following restrictions apply to files uploaded as part of this application process:

o File format must be in JPG, PDF, TXT, RTF, DOC, DOCX or WPD;
o File size must not exceed three (3) megabytes; and
o File(s) must not include macros or scripts of any kind.

Note: Faxed applications and/or résumés will not be accepted.

To begin the process,

1. Click the **Apply Online** button to create an account or sign in to your existing USAJOBS account.
2. Follow the prompts to create or select your USAJOBS résumé and be routed to the *Application Manager* system.
3. Complete the online Assessment Questionnaire.
4. For your answers to be processed, you must click the **Submit My Answers** button.

Important Technical Note: Please note that you must complete/submit your application in Application Manager before the ALJ Job Opportunity Announcement closes at 11:59 pm ET on Friday, March 15, 2013. After the Announcement is closed, you will not be able to complete/submit your application.

Also note that Application Manager has a **timeout** feature for security purposes that will log a user out of the system after a certain period of inactivity. To preserve your work in Application Manager, it is very important that you use the **SAVE** button approximately every 10 minutes. The system also saves your work every time you click the **NEXT** button. If you do not save your work and the system times you out, you will lose any information entered since your last use of **SAVE/NEXT** and you will have to log back in to Application Manager. You will see a pop up warning message asking if you need more time before the timeout occurs.

Technical Problems

If you have technical problems concerning this application process, please send an email to aljapplication@opm.gov. Such inquiries must include your name as it appears on your online application/assessment questionnaire in order to properly identify your record and address your issue. Your submission of an inquiry does not automatically change the response deadline for any part of the ALJ application process. Substantive questions concerning an individual application will not be answered as to do so would give an unfair advantage in the examination process.

Online Application and Assessment Questionnaire

Social Security Number

Enter your Social Security Number. Providing your Social Security Number is voluntary. We cannot process your application without it, however. The authority for soliciting and verifying your Social Security Number is Executive Order 9397.

Vacancy Identification Number

ALJ2013-847661

Title of Job

Administrative Law Judge

Biographic Data

E-Mail Address

Spanish Fluency

Can you speak and write Spanish at a level equivalent to native proficiency and are you able to communicate effectively, both orally and in writing, in Spanish and English in order to translate documents, converse and ask questions with counsel, provide explanations, understand testimony by claimants and conduct hearings in Spanish?

Sole Survivorship Veterans' Preference

Pursuant to 5 U.S.C. § 2108(3)(H), certain veterans discharged or released from a period of active duty from the armed forces by reason of sole survivorship are considered preference eligibles. Under sole survivorship preference, the veteran does not receive veterans' preference points, but is entitled to be listed ahead of non-preference eligibles with the same score; is entitled to receive the same pass-over rights as other preference eligibles during selection; and is entitled to credit experience in the armed forces to meet qualifications requirements. The service member must be released or discharged from the armed forces under honorable conditions, following a qualifying period of service, after August 29, 2008, at the request of the member who is the only surviving child in a family in which the father or mother or one or more siblings (1) served in the armed forces; (2) was killed, died as a result of wounds, accident, or disease, is in a captured or missing in action status, or is permanently 100 percent disabled or hospitalized on a continuing basis (and is not employed gainfully because of the disability or hospitalization); and (3) death, status, or disability did not result from the intentional misconduct or willful neglect of the parent or sibling and was not incurred during a period of unauthorized absence.

Applicants seeking sole survivorship preference must respond "Yes" to the following question.

Do you claim veterans' preference based on having been released or discharged from a period of active duty from the armed forces, after August 29, 2008, by reason of sole survivorship?

Citizenship

Are you a citizen of the United States?

Lowest Level

The level for this position is: AL-3.

Reasonable Accommodation for SJT/Writing Sample/Experience Assessment

OPM provides reasonable accommodation for the SJT, Writing Sample, and/or Experience Assessment parts of the examination to applicants with disabilities, where appropriate, for the purpose of providing equivalent access to the examination process. Accommodations may include such modifications as changes in the presentation format, response format, assessment setting, timing, or scheduling. Determinations on requests for accommodation(s) will be made on a case-by-case basis and must be approved prior to starting the SJT, Writing Sample, and/or Experience Assessment parts of the ALJ examination. If you need an accommodation(s) with the SJT, Writing Sample, and/or Experience Assessment, please respond "Yes" to the following question. You will be contacted to obtain additional information and to make special testing arrangements, if appropriate.

Do you require an accommodation(s) with the SJT, Writing Sample, and/or Experience Assessment?

Veteran Preference Claim

Applicants entitled to veterans' preference (other than sole survivorship preference) must submit the appropriate documentation of release or discharge, or expectation of imminent release or discharge, by the closing date of the ALJ Job Opportunity Announcement as described below.

Five (5) Point Veterans' Preference:

Applicants claiming 5-point veterans' preference, who are no longer in the military service, must submit a DD Form 214, Certificate of Release or Discharge from Active Duty, or other documentation that provides equivalent information on the length and type of service and the character of release or discharge.

Applicants who are still in the military service during this ALJ Job Opportunity Announcement's open period may be granted 5-point preference when a written statement/certification is submitted certifying the service member is expected to be discharged or released from active duty service in the armed forces under honorable conditions within 120 days after submission.

Supporting documentation for 5 point veterans' preference will not be accepted after the closing date of the announcement.

Applicants who claimed preference pursuant to a statement/certification that they expect to be discharged or released within 120 days must provide a DD Form 214, or other documentation that provides equivalent information on the length and type of service and the character of release or discharge, to the hiring agency at the time of appointment, to confirm discharge or release and entitlement to veterans' preference.

Ten (10) Point Veterans' Preference for Current and Former Service Members:

Applicants claiming 10-point veterans' preference on the basis of their own service, who are no longer in the military service, must submit a DD Form 214, Certificate of Release or Discharge from Active Duty, or one of the other forms of documentation of service and separation under honorable conditions that OPM has outlined in the SF-15, Application for 10-Point Veteran Preference, page 2, table A, available at http://www.opm.gov/forms/. This documentation is needed to establish character of service. They must also submit documentation of service-connected disability, as described at page 2, table B or C of the SF-15.

Applicants claiming 10-point veterans' preference on the basis of their own service, who are still in the military service during this ALJ Job Opportunity Announcement's open period may be granted preference when a written statement/certification is submitted certifying the service member is expected to be discharged or released from active duty service in the armed forces under honorable conditions within 120 days after submission. In order to obtain the full 10 points, such applicants must also submit documentation of service-connected disability, as described at page 2, table B or C of the SF-15, Application for 10-Point Veteran Preference, available at http://www.opm.gov/forms/.

If, during the open period, an applicant claiming 10-point veterans' preference on the basis of his or her own service does not submit documentation of service-connected disability but does submit documentation establishing discharge or release (or imminent discharge or release as described above) and character of service, he or she will be awarded 5-point preference, based on the documentation submitted, until proof is submitted to support the service-connected disability. Appropriate documentation of service-connected disability may be submitted after the closing date, but must be submitted electronically to aljapplication@opm.gov. Faxed documents or those sent through the postal or other delivery service will not be accepted. Such applicants must provide a DD Form 214, or one of the other forms of documentation of service and separation under honorable conditions that OPM has identified, to the hiring agency at the time of appointment, to confirm separation and entitlement to veterans' preference.

Ten (10) Point Veterans' Preference for Spouses, Widows, Widowers, and Mothers of Veterans:

Applicants claiming 10-point veterans' preference on the basis of being the spouse, widow, widower, or mother of a service member must submit a completed SF-15, Application for 10-Point Veteran Preference, available at http://www.opm.gov/forms/, with the supporting documents specified by the form.

For more information on Veterans' Preference, please visit http://www.fedshirevets.gov/.

Please select the appropriate veterans' preference claim (unless you claimed veterans' preference based on a sole survivorship discharge).

NV: No Preference Claimed.
TP: 5 Points Preference Claimed.
XP: 10 Points Preference Claimed (award of a Purple Heart or compensable service-connected disability of less than 10% or, 10 Points Other (wife, widow, husband, widower, mother preference claimed)).
CP: 10 Points Compensable Disability Preference Claimed (disability rating of at least 10% and less than 30%).
CPS: 10 Points Compensable Disability Preference Claimed (disability rating of 30% or more).

Dates of Active Duty - Military Service

Occupational Specialties

001 Administrative Law Judge

Geographic Availability

Please carefully select the geographical locations where you would be willing to accept an appointment as an ALJ by an agency of the Federal Government. Once this ALJ Job Opportunity Announcement closes, you will not be able to change (i.e., add or remove) your selected geographical location(s) until the next ALJ Job Opportunity Announcement open period. OPM may announce additional periods during which candidates already on the register may make changes, at OPM's discretion.

If, after selecting your geographical location(s), you decline consideration for a geographical location for which you indicated availability, you will be removed from further consideration for that location. You will not be able to reinstate a location from which you have been removed until the next ALJ Job Opportunity Announcement open period.

Locations:

020130020 Anchorage, AK
010350073 Birmingham, AL
011200077 Florence, AL
012100097 Mobile, AL
012130101 Montgomery, AL
051370131 Fort Smith, AR
052320119 Little Rock, AR
040370013 Phoenix, AZ
040530019 Tucson, AZ
060010001 Alameda, CA
061370019 Fresno, CA
061713059 Irvine, CA
061970037 Long Beach, CA
061980037 Los Angeles, CA

[Location info redacted}

Assessment Questionnaire:

1. Do you have a full seven (7) years of experience as a licensed attorney preparing for, participating in, and/or reviewing formal hearings or trials involving litigation and/or administrative law at the Federal, State or local level?

NOTE: If you fail to respond or if you answer "No" to the questions in this section, or if you do not provide sufficient information to show that you will pass the preliminary qualifications screening, you will be rated as "ineligible." We will not request or accept any additional information and/or clarification beyond what you provide in the following text boxes.

A. Yes
B. No

If your answer is "Yes," in order to document that you meet this experience requirement, in the following two text boxes you must fully describe the amount of time spent performing these activities as well as your actual experience in litigation and/or administrative law work.

Your response will be evaluated to determine if you pass the preliminary qualifications screening, and the extent to which your responses to this questionnaire show that you possess the competencies, or knowledge, skills and abilities, associated with the ALJ position. When you are describing your experience, it is extremely important that you provide sufficient detail to show that you have completed, in the aggregate, a full seven years of qualifying experience. Therefore, you must quantify the time associated with any claimed experience in terms of the specific dates it was acquired, including the month and year for the start and end dates, such as May 2006-December 2006. Also, if you provide an example of qualifying experience that overlaps with other non-qualifying experience, you must provide the percentage of time spent on each type of work.

In the text box below, describe your experience, if applicable, that relates to the "litigation experience" requirements as defined in the "Qualifications Requirements" section. Please pay special attention to the above instructions concerning specificity and detail.

2. All ALJ applicants are required to certify that they are duly licensed to practice law as an attorney at the time of filing, under the laws of a State, the District of Columbia, the Commonwealth of Puerto Rico, or any territorial court established under the United States Constitution. Judicial status is acceptable in lieu of "active" status in States that prohibit sitting Judges from maintaining "active" status to practice law. Being in "good standing" is acceptable in lieu of "active" status in States where the licensing authority considers "good standing" as having a current license to practice law.

Do you meet these licensure requirements?

A. Yes – As described above, I hereby certify that I am duly licensed to practice law at the time of the filing of this application for employment as an ALJ, under the laws of a State, the District of Columbia, the Commonwealth of Puerto Rico, or any territorial court established under the United States Constitution.

B. Yes -- As described above, I hereby certify that I am in a judicial status at the time of the filing of this application for employment as an ALJ, and that my licensing jurisdiction prohibits me, as a sitting judge, from maintaining an "active" status to practice law.

C. No – As described above, I do not certify that I am duly licensed to practice law at the time of the filing of this application for employment as an ALJ or that I am a sitting judge who is required by my licensing jurisdiction to be in a judicial status.

If you answered "Yes" (item 2.A or 2.B), use the text box below to list: a) all jurisdictions in which you are currently licensed to practice law; b) the date(s) of admission to the Bar in each jurisdiction in which you are currently licensed to practice law; (c) the Bar license number in each jurisdiction in which you are currently licensed to practice law; and (d) if you maintain a bar status other than active, please explain your status, and specify the jurisdiction in which you have this status. If a State in which you are licensed to practice law does not issue a Bar license number, you must clearly state this fact in the text box below and still provide the remaining requested information.

An applicant could be deemed ineligible at any time if it is determined that he/she does not satisfy or ceases to satisfy the licensure requirement.

3. Reasonable Accommodation for WD/LBM Test/SI

OPM provides reasonable accommodation for the Written Demonstration (WD), Logic-Based Measurement Test (LBMT), and Structured Interview (SI) components of the examination to applicants with disabilities, where appropriate, for the purpose of providing equivalent access to the examination process. Accommodations may include such modifications as changes in the presentation format, response format, assessment setting, timing, or scheduling. Determinations on requests for accommodation(s) will be made on a case-by-case basis and must be approved prior to participating in the WD, LBMT and/or SI parts of the ALJ examination. If you need an accommodation(s) with the WD, LBMT and/or SI, please respond "Yes" to the following question. You will be contacted to obtain additional information and to make special testing arrangements, if appropriate.

Do you require an accommodation(s) with the WD, LBMT and/or SI?

4. Certification of Information Accuracy

I *certify* that, to the best of my knowledge and belief, all of the information included in this Assessment Questionnaire is true, correct, and provided in good faith. I *understand* that if I make an intentional false statement, or commit deception or fraud in this application and its supporting materials, or in any document or interview associated with the examination and appointment process, I may be fined or imprisoned (18 U.S.C. 1001); my eligibilities may be cancelled, I may be denied an appointment, or I may be removed and/or debarred from the Federal service (5 CFR part 731); or I may be disciplined under applicable state law by the authorities responsible for regulating the conduct of attorneys and judges. I *understand* that any information I give may be investigated. I *understand* that I will be rated "ineligible" if I do not respond "Yes" to this certification item, or if I fail to respond at all to this certification item.

A. Yes, I certify/understand the information provided above.
B. No, I do not certify/understand the information provided above.

REQUIRED DOCUMENTS:

- Résumé; and
- Veterans' Preference documentation (if you are claiming Veterans' Preference)

Optional Document:

- **OPTIONAL LISTING OF SIGNIFICANT LITIGATION AND/OR ADMINISTRATIVE LAW CASES**

AGENCY CONTACT INFO:

Admin Law Judge Program Office
Phone: (000)000-0000
Email: ALJAPPLICATION@OPM.GOV

Agency Information:
Administrative Law Judge Exam
No Specific Address
None, DC
00000

WHAT TO EXPECT NEXT:

Once you submit your Application Package, you will be sent an email acknowledging your submission. The acknowledgement email, however, does not establish eligibility to proceed to the remaining parts of the ALJ examination. Please refer to the **Basis for Rating** section of this ALJ Job Opportunity Announcement for specific information about the notification process regarding the evaluation of your questionnaire, and if applicable, the details about the remaining parts of the examination. The ALJ assessment and examination process is comprehensive and requires an extended period of time for the process to be completed for all the applicants who applied during the announcement open period. Final numerical ratings will not be issued until the assessment and examination process has been completed for all applicants who applied during the open period.

NOTE: ALJ inquiries must be sent to the ALJ mailbox at aljapplication@opm.gov. OPM staff will not respond to telephone inquiries or emails sent directly to them.

Additional Duty Location Info
Many vacancies in the following locations:
Santa Barbara, CA United States   View Map   [Location info redacted}

APPENDIX B

Special Hiring Considerations: Schedule A, Veterans, and 10-Point Veterans

Unlike federal 0905 series attorney positions, 0935 ALJ series jobs are not Excepted Service. Thus 5- and 10-point Veterans can have these points added to their scores. Veterans can also count their military service towards their qualifying experience. The 2013 announcement explained:

> For applicants entitled to veterans' preference, time spent in the Armed Forces of the United States shall be considered as qualifying experience in either of the two following ways, depending upon which will be more beneficial to applicants:
>
> 1. Such service may be considered on the basis of actual duties performed by the applicant as an attorney or military judge in the military services, or
>
> 2. Such service may be considered as an extension of the employment in which the applicant was engaged immediately before entrance into the military service. When military service is credited in this way, the applicant is considered to have continued performing the duties of the position he/she left.

In addition, 10-point Veterans, as defined in 5 U.S.C. §§2108(3)(C)-(G) and 3309(1), are entitled to apply to closed exams.[1] However, as the testing period for the 2013 announcement has concluded, OPM will likely instruct 10-point Veterans and Schedule A candidates not to apply to the 2013 announcement, but to wait for the 2016 exam.

Those unable to file for an open competitive examination because of military service may file after the closing date. In either case, the veteran should contact OPM for further information.

Likewise, qualified applicants with Schedule A disabilities are entitled to apply to closed exams.[2]

---

1 See http://www.fedshirevets.gov/BLOG/FHVNews/2012/5/4/OPM-Posts-Notice-to-10-Point-Preference-Eligible-Veterans-Regarding-the-ALJ-Examination/.
2 See http://www.fedshirevets.gov/job/shav/#scheda.

Appendix C

Frequently Asked Questions

When will the ALJ Announcement be posted?

The Bipartisan Budget Act of 2015, which passed on November 2, 2015, requires the testing to begin no later than April 1, 2016. Although the announcement could be posted anytime, there will probably be at least a 2-week warning. In 2009, a press release was issued nearly two weeks in advance. In 2013, OPM released news of the upcoming announcement approximately one month ahead of time. The 2016 OPM news release will likely be posted here: https://www.opm.gov/news/latest-news/.

Do I need prior judicial experience?

No. Most ALJs were not judges beforehand, although former state and local judges do well in the process. Perhaps half of all Social Security ALJs have no prior SSA experience, but statistics suggest roughly half come into the process from ODAR or from the private disability bar. To debunk another myth, no political connections are required. ALJs are the only U.S. judges appointed solely on merit. They are rated and ranked based on the information provided in the published exam process.

Will the exam close after a certain number of applications are received?

When the announcement is posted, the application will be open for the designated period of time. In 2013, OPM advised that the number of applications would not be limited as in prior years. Instead, all applications received within the specified filing period were processed. In comparison, only 600 applications were allowed in 2008, and that number was reached on the second day the announcement was posted. In 2009, 700 applications were received in 30 hours. As of this writing, it is not yet known how long the new announcement will remain open.

What are keywords and do I need to worry about them?

Keywords are the concept words and phrases that pertain to the minimum qualifications and required competencies for the job. They can be found right in the announcement and assessment questions. Because the resumes are read by humans, not machines, the repetitive use of specific buzz words is unnecessary. However, the careful use of language mirroring the specific qualifications and competencies laid out in the announcement will help reviewers focus in on your relevant experience and the knowledge, skills and abilities you possess. Remember that the use of legal jargon and complicated language can hurt your application, which will be read, in the first instance, by non-lawyers at OPM.

Do you have to be an agency insider to have a real shot at this job?

No. Each applicant is rated solely on merit and qualifications. In fact, being an agency insider can be a detriment if your work is viewed as less than stellar. By the time of your structured interview, interviewers will have gained access to your entire agency history.

Where can I find the 2009 ALJ announcement?

OPM withdrew the 2009 announcement, but a facsimile may still be found in the documents library of the Federal Administrative Law Judges Conference. This library is open to FALJC members only, but copy of the announcement, as posted by FALJC on its website back in 2009, is maintained on www.archive.org. You can access it by pasting this dead link into archive.org's http search bar: http://005754d.netsolhost.com/faljc7.html.

Where can I find a list of the agencies that hire ALJs?

The 34 agencies that hire ALJs are listed here: http://www.aalj.org/agencies-employing-administrative-law-judges.

How much are ALJs are paid?

The ALJ pay system has three basic levels: AL-1, AL-2, and AL-3. AL-3 is the basic level for ALJ positions filled through competitive examination and has six rates: A, B, C, D, E, and F. AL-2 and AL-1 pay is set by agencies subject to OPM's approval. ALJ positions are set at AL-2 and AL-1 if they involve significant administrative or management duties.

Here are the 2016 ALJ salaries for various localities: http://www.opm.gov/policy-data-oversight/pay-leave/salaries-wages/salary-tables/pdf/2016/ALJ_LOC.pdf. The overall fact sheet for ALJ pay system is here: https://www.opm.gov/policy-data-oversight/pay-leave/pay-administration/fact-sheets/administrative-law-judge-pay-system/.

Is there a fixed set of qualifications for ALJs?

Yes. OPM is in charge of it: https://www.opm.gov/policy-data-oversight/classification-qualifications/general-schedule-qualification-standards/specialty-areas/administrative-law-judge-positions/.

What other relevant documents are online?

November 12, 2015 ALJ Work Analysis Study:
https://drive.google.com/file/d/0B2kAAfgH45ClZjRGejdwSkwyNXc.

Bipartisan Budget Act of 2015: https://www.congress.gov/bill/114th-congress/house-bill/1314.

SSA Office of the Inspector General Reports:

2015 Fall Semiannual Report to Congress –
http://oig.ssa.gov/sites/default/files/semiannual/Semiannual%20Fall%202015.pdf.

Audit Report: The Social Security Administration's Efforts to Eliminate the Hearings Backlog, September 23, 2015 – http://oig.ssa.gov/sites/default/files/audit/full/pdf/A-12-15-15005.pdf.

Are there professional organizations for ALJs?

The Federal Administrative Law Judges Conference (FALJC) is a 60+ year old professional association that seeks to improve the administrative judicial process, presents educational programs, and represents ALJs' concerns in matters affecting the administrative judiciary. Membership includes Judges from every agency that employs ALJs. FAJLC speaks out on behalf of its members on issues relating to the administrative judicial process and issues regarding the status of ALJs as Federal employees: http://www.faljc.org/.

The Association of Administrative Law Judges (AALJ) was founded as a professional association in 1971. In 1999, AALJ chose to affiliate with the International Federation of Professional and Technical Engineers, AFL-CIO, joining other federal judges and professional employees. Their website states that 80+ percent of SSA judges are active members of AALJ: http://www.aalj.org/.

The National Association of Administrative Law Judiciary (NAALJ), founded in 1974, is the largest professional organization devoted exclusively to administrative adjudication in the executive branch of government: http://www.naalj.org/.

What about blogs and social media?

Social Security Blog (tagged for ALJs):
http://socsecnews.blogspot.com/search/label/ALJs.

ALJ Discussion Forum:
http://aljdiscussion.proboards.com/.

Appendix D

Example of Accomplishment Writing in Other Federal Adjudicatory Positions

Sample assessment question from Federal Hearing Officer Announcement (Series 0930):

INSTRUCTIONS FOR ACCOMPLISHMENT NARRATIVE:

Submit Accomplishment Record:

Prepare and submit a written narrative of a maximum of one (1) page in length describing a specific instance from your training and/or experience in which you demonstrated experience in Legal, Government and Jurisprudence, as described below:

Legal, Government, and Jurisprudence - Hearing Officers are expected to do the following in relation to Legal, Government, and Jurisprudence:

• Demonstrate technical expertise in the areas of laws, legal codes, court procedures, precedents, legal practices and documents, government regulations, executive orders, agency rules, government organization and functions, and the democratic political process.

• Apply technical knowledge independently to develop sound and accurate conclusions.

Prepare and submit your accomplishment in one document. Upload this document in Application Manager using the Qualifications option in the drop down menu.

You may choose to describe paid work experience, education, training, volunteer work experience, hobbies, or any other accomplishment. Your accomplishment should focus on one specific incident or example. Multiple examples will not be considered; only the first situation will be rated.

Your accomplishment cannot exceed one page in length. To ensure consistency in the length requirements of documents, the sample MUST be in a 12-point font, single spaced. Any additional information beyond one page will not be evaluated.

In your response, follow these important guidelines as you write your accomplishment. Include the following information:

• Describe the SITUATION – a general statement of the situation or circumstances surrounding what you accomplished/achieved (i.e., the challenge faced, the problem to be solved, or the objective to be achieved -as it relates to the competency being addressed)

• Describe the specific ACTIONS – a precise description of exactly what you did (i.e., activities you performed, duties, and responsibilities) in your own words. Do not quote someone else describing what you did. The actions you describe are particularly important in evaluating your accomplishment.

• State the OUTCOMES – a description of the outcomes (the direct or indirect results or long-term impact of your accomplishment)

• The start and end dates of the time period during which the activities were performed. Please be specific and provide the month and year for the start and end dates (e.g., June 2006 to November 2006).

• The name and a telephone number or email address or other method of contacting someone who can verify the information you provide. Be sure to indicate whether this person was your supervisor, co-worker, friend, instructor, chairman of a committee, etc. If you do not want your current employer contacted, do not list your employer as a verifying person. Instead, provide the name of another person who can verify your accomplishment. Do not use a spouse or a close relative (father, mother, etc.) or a person who is presently a direct subordinate as a verifier. The verifier must be reachable within a reasonable period. You MUST provide a reference for verification of your Accomplishment Record. If you do not provide a reference, your Accomplishment Record will NOT be read or evaluated. Please note that once the Accomplishment Record has been evaluated, verifiers may or may not be contacted.

NICOLE SCHULTHEIS

Nicole Schultheis has helped hundreds of attorneys and other senior candidates compete successfully for federal positions. In addition to Administrative Law Judge candidates, she has helped aspiring Administrative Judges, Hearing Officers, Immigration Judges and Administrative Patent Judges. She has supported legal and law enforcement candidates at the Department of Justice, FBI, ICE, CBP, DHS, U.S. Secret Service, U.S. Department of Defense, as well as applicants to numerous agency Offices of General Counsel, Inspectors General, and Legislative Counsel offices.

She has conducted trainings and given workshops on federal resume writing and executive writing for lawyers and other professionals. She teaches autobiographical writing to continuing education students at Anne Arundel Community College, Arnold, Maryland, and is a past president of the Maryland Writers' Association.

Schultheis is also a former appellate judicial clerk and a trial lawyer with significant state and federal trial and appellate experience. She has contributed chapters on litigation subjects to legal treatises, and her articles have been published in The Maryland Daily Record, Maryland Bar Journal, Maryland Journal of Contemporary Legal Issues, and elsewhere.

Schultheis holds a Bachelor of Science in biology from the Massachusetts Institute of Technology and a Juris Doctor from Boston University School of Law. Since 2005, she has maintained an AV Preeminent® rating from Martindale Hubbell, their highest possible rating, earned by only 5 percent of all female attorneys. She is a member of the Maryland bar.

KATHRYN TROUTMAN

Kathryn Troutman is the founder and president of The Resume Place Inc., located in Baltimore, Md., and specializes in writing and designing professional federal and private-sector resumes, as well as coaching and education in the federal hiring process. For more than 30 years, Troutman has managed her professional writing and consulting practice, publishing, and federal career training business, and, with her team of 20 Certified Federal Resume Writers, The Resume Place advises and writes more than 300 federal resumes per month for military, private industry, and federal clients worldwide.

Internationally recognized as the "Federal Resume Guru" by federal human resources specialists and jobseekers, Troutman created the format and name for the new "federal resume" that became an accepted standard after the SF 171 form was discontinued in 1995. She is the pioneering designer of the federal resume based on her first book, the *Federal Resume Guidebook*, now in its sixth edition. Some of Troutman's other federal career publications include the award-winning *Student's Federal Career Guide (Third Edition), Ten Steps to a Federal Job (Third Edition), Jobseeker's Guide (Seventh Edition),* and the *Military to Federal Career Guide (Second Edition),* which is used in every Navy and Marine Corps base in the world, as well as most Air Force career transition centers.

A frequent radio, TV, and online guest, Troutman answers questions about federal careers, resume writing, and job search techniques. Troutman currently serves as Monster.com's Federal Career Coach, where she writes a monthly column. She has been quoted and published hundreds of times on the topic of federal resume writing and job searching through syndicated news articles by Joyce Lain Kennedy and numerous career columnists. Troutman is a frequent guest on washingtonpost.com's Federal Diary Live Online and federalnewsradio.com.

Troutman is a member of Professional Association of Résumé Writers, National Résumé Writer's Association, Independent Book Publishers Association, and the Association of Women Business Owners.

ALj Writing / Consulting Services

Application Preparation for the 2016 Announcement

Our full service package includes the following components:

- Federal ALJ-style, outline format resume for upload to www.USAJOBS.gov (typically 3–5 pages)

- Two qualifications narratives, documenting 7+ years of qualifying litigation and administrative law experience

- Two hours of phone consulting/coaching, spread over the project

- A homework assignment in accomplishment/past performance writing, addressing ALJ competencies

- An electronic copy of the all new ALJ Writing Guide, 2nd Edition, by Nicole Schultheis & Kathryn Troutman (2016)

- A selection of additional written materials to assist with exam preparation

Additional Optional Services:

- Developmental Editing and Proofreading of the optional Listing of Cases

- Structured Interview preparation and recorded mock interview

- Additional preparation services may also be added, depending upon the requirements of the 2016 ALJ Announcement and exam.

For More Information & Assistance
www.resume-place.com/alj